CODEWORDS

Dr Gareth Moore B.Sc (Hons) M.Phil Ph.D is the internationally best-selling author of a wide range of brain-training and puzzle books for both children and adults, including *Enigma: Crack the Code*, *Ultimate Dot to Dot*, *Brain Games for Clever Kids*, *Lateral Logic* and *Extreme Mazes*. His books have sold millions of copies in the UK alone, and have been published in over thirty different languages. He is also the creator of online brain-training site BrainedUp.com, and runs the daily puzzle site PuzzleMix.com.

Web: DrGarethMoore.com
Twitter: @DrGarethMoore
YouTube: YouTube.com/@DrGareth

Perfect Pocket Puzzles

CODEWORDS

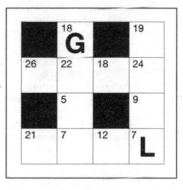

Dr Gareth Moore

Michael O'Mara Books Limited

First published in Great Britain in 2024 by
Michael O'Mara Books Limited
9 Lion Yard
Tremadoc Road
London SW4 7NQ

Copyright © Michael O'Mara Books Limited 2024
Puzzles and solutions copyright © Dr Gareth Moore 2024

A CIP catalogue record for this book is available from the British Library.

Papers used by Michael O'Mara Books Limited are natural, recyclable products made
from wood grown in sustainable forests. The manufacturing processes conform to the
environmental regulations of the country of origin.

ISBN: 978-1-78929-607-5 in paperback print format

1 2 3 4 5 6 7 8 9 10

Designed by Gareth Moore

Printed and bound by CPI Group (UK) Ltd, Croydon, CR0 4YY

www.mombooks.com

		4		9		4		18		25		23
	11	8	13	4	11	17		1	26	4	20 T	19
		13		14		4	22	1		3		18
9	17	4	11	23	11			11	25	4	20	19
26			25				14		1		19	
19	16	7	6	26 R	19		4	12	6	26	19	
2		11			24	26	15			19		19
	4	6	23	19	24		11	13	26	21	19	15
	11		1		15				19			19
7	17	6	4 I	14			5	13	24	22	19	24
1		9		1	12	12		11		1		
24	2	19	19	10		1	7	19	26	4	11	
11		24		19		7		11		14		

A	B	C	D	E	F	G	H	I	J	K	L	M
N	O	P	Q	R	S	T	U	V	W	X	Y	Z

1	2	3	4	5	6	7	8	9	10	11	12	13
14	15	16	17	18	19	20	21	22	23	24	25	26

Codeword 2

	21	14	18	8	15	2	12		5	25	25	12
26		5		11		22			20		10	**S**
21	14	11	22	25		21	7	21	23	22	21	12
2		2		5		26		11			13	
14	5	10	3		26	5	23	19	1	21	2	24
24		21		16		2		20		11 **N**		
	12	14	10	21	26		26	21	8	12	22	
		2		23		12		19		20		12
21	16	12	5	23	8	2	22		2 **T**	22	6	2
	21			5		21		9		10		5
26	12	21	23	2	22	10		21	25	15	22	8
	15		22			17		15		11		2
21	14	22	25		4	22	5	23	5	4	19	

A B C D E F G H I J K L M
N O P Q R S T U V W X Y Z

1	2	3	4	5	6	7	8	9	10	11	12	13

14	15	16	17	18	19	20	21	22	23	24	25	26

Codeword 3

	9		20		10		4		5		16	
26	12	7	10	18	17		15	19	24	19	25	14
	25		4		19		12		20		10	
21	10	4	1		12	1	1	6	25	20	5	7
	16				18		2		12		22	
18	6	18	9	8	12	15	12	18	9	5		
	19		6						20		25	
	5	2	16	12	25	25	12	1	1	5	1	
	14		4		15		8				13	
11	5	15	6	9	10	20	14		15	5	5	23
	15		1		17		2		6		9	
1	4	5	5	9	8		5	3	19	12	20	5
	1		1		20		7		20		1	

Grid letters shown: O (at 6), A (at 12), D (at 7)

A	B	C	D	E	F	G	H	I	J	K	L	M
N	O	P	Q	R	S	T	U	V	W	X	Y	Z

1	2	3	4	5	6	7	8	9	10	11	12	13
14	15	16	17	18	19	20	21	22	23	24	25	26

17	20	14	11	7	14	■	1	9	24	15	9	1
9	■	18	■	24	■	20	■	5	■	7	■	20
21	4	6	14	11	7	14	■	25	16	9	5	24
21	■	7	■	7	■	3	■	6	■	3	■	7
■	2	7	20	15	■	7	20	15	4	9 **I**	7	15
14	■	22	■	■	■	8	■	7	■	■	■	9
6	5	7	19	7	5	■	20	14	14	9	2	5
17	■	■	■	26	■	17	■	■	■	5	■	2
14	16	12 **M**	7	16	5	7	■	15	16	19	7	■
9	■	7	■	24	■	7	■	16	■	16	■	9
14	6	14	11	9	■	1	16	6	23 **P**	4	7	14
24	■	16	■	1	■	11	■	5	■	19	■	4
14	13	5	24	20	26	■	20	10	11	7	15	7

A	B	C	D	E	F	G	H	I	J	K	L	M
N	O	P	Q	R	S	T	U	V	W	X	Y	Z

1	2	3	4	5	6	7	8	9	10	11	12	13
14	15	16	17	18	19	20	21	22	23	24	25	26

Codeword 5

	20		7		1		19		24		2	
2	11	20	9	5	6		15	22	16	16	23	19
	2		23		13	23	17		23 **A**		12	
21	22	20	20	5	6		22		17	23	15	19
	4				5	23	12				22	
21	11	24	9	19 **S**		13		6	18	15	6	5
		26		6	4	23	24	14		17		
11	5	22	10	6		8		23	12	11	4	3
	9			15	6	17				23		
25	17	22	12		26		23	5	14	6	17	19
	8	**I**	17		11	17	25		6		17	
17	6	19	22	12	4		25	6	23	24	11	4
	20		2		6		22		17		13	

A	B	C	D	E	F	G	H	I	J	K	L	M
N	O	P	Q	R	S	T	U	V	W	X	Y	Z

1	2	3	4	5	6	7	8	9	10	11	12	13
14	15	16	17	18	19	20	21	22	23	24	25	26

Codeword 6

4	13	18	4	13	22	■	19	20	4	15	13	26
■	6	■	2	■	20	■	20	■	17	■	4	■
26	21	26	3	■	23	26	25	4	19	13 **L**	24	11
■	26	■	6	■	26	■	6	■	4	■	26	■
24	3	4	20	11	25	26	3	■	24	6	3	26
■	26	■	■	■	4	■	24	■	22	■	■	■
4	23	7	19	11	24	■	19	20	5	13	4	23
■	■	■	24	■	22	■	20	■	■	■	5	■
24	4	8	22	■	14	3	4	2	1	22 **I**	5	11
■	14	■	13	■	4	■	24	■	6	■	19	■
12	4	3 **R**	22	4	15	13	26	■	3	6	11	9
■	22	■	24	■	13	■	13	■	23	■	26	■
26	20	16	9	10	26	■	9	22	26	13	23	11

A	B	C	D	E	F	G	H	I	J	K	L	M
N	O	P	Q	R	S	T	U	V	W	X	Y	Z

1	2	3	4	5	6	7	8	9	10	11	12	13
14	15	16	17	18	19	20	21	22	23	24	25	26

Codeword 7

1	21	8	20	■	20	■	2	■	20	15	9	1
8	■	16	■	14	9	26	7	15	■	19	■	9
5	4	4	3	■	25	■	8	■	1	21	15	20
20	■	17	8	10	4	■	15	8	16	20	■	20
■	13	■	10	■	20	7	4	■	15	■	20	■
13	9	7	14	19	15	■	11	18	4	9	26	20
■	18	■	■	4	■	■	■	4	■	■	8 (O)	■
15	18	9	21	10	20	■	4	25	25	4	13	15
■	16	■	10	■	5	4	9	■	3	■	6	■
19	■	8	6	18	9	■	20	23	9	14	■	14
4	10	12	16	■	13	■	21	■	6	9	3 (L)	4
3	■	4	■	22	4 (E)	3	3	16	■	18	■	10
26	21	10	24	■	20	■	16	■	9	1	3	4

A	B	C	D	E	F	G	H	I	J	K	L	M
N	O	P	Q	R	S	T	U	V	W	X	Y	Z

1	2	3	4	5	6	7	8	9	10	11	12	13
14	15	16	17	18	19	20	21	22	23	24	25	26

Codeword 8

1	12	9	5	23		9	4	7	26	14	22	15
	15		3		13		23		5		12	
7	8	15	26	3	4	12	14		15	24	3	18 **M**
	3		26		3		6		15		14	
9	1	7	3	14	23		15	3	7	15	23 **N**	
			14		7		12				15	
12	15	15	2		14	17	26		1	3	22	15
	10				20		14		9			
	15	24	7	12	3		7	12	9	9	19	26
	11		15		7		14		21		3	
26	7	4	23		14	22	15	9	2	9	16	25
	15		15		9		26		15		15	
15	22 **D**	14	7	14	23	16		26	7	3	26	8

A	B	C	D	E	F	G	H	I	J	K	L	M
N	O	P	Q	R	S	T	U	V	W	X	Y	Z

1	2	3	4	5	6	7	8	9	10	11	12	13
14	15	16	17	18	19	20	21	22	23	24	25	26

Codeword 9

	25		17		19		3		10		
16	17	8	22	21		12	13	**20** U	18	17	22
19		22		6		4		17		2		6
18	13	8	22	19	9	7		13	17	2	19	13
8		18		18		21		13				8
6	19	17	15		19		5	4	11	17	16	18
4		16		19	23	23	17	22		22		8
17	**13** R	18	8	21	18		1		12	22	19	6
12			18		21		19		8		8
22	19	24	4	13		5	8	2	2	17	2	2
7		4		8 **I**		17		19		16		4
	18	13	20	6	26	21		16	8	6	26	21
	7		14		25		4		4		

A	B	C	D	E	F	G	H	I	J	K	L	M
N	O	P	Q	R	S	T	U	V	W	X	Y	Z

1	2	3	4	5	6	7	8	9	10	11	12	13
14	15	16	17	18	19	20	21	22	23	24	25	26

	5		10		6		6		6		17
9	26	23	21	6	18		18	24	25	26	14	6
	14		9		26	17	11		24		11	
7	17 (**I**)	13	26	11	20		24		9	21	24	2
	14				16	8	8				6	
3	17	14	16	6		17		5	26	2	18	6
		16		18	17	14	2	6		26 (**A**)		
15	24	16	11	10		20		17	14	20	16	12
	5				22	17	20				1	
26	6	5	6		21		11	16	14	20	16	11
	17		19		7	21	21		16		4	
26	20	22	17	4	16		7	16	26	23	2 (**T**)	18
	16		6		23		14		2		6	

A B C D E F G H I J K L M
N O P Q R S T U V W X Y Z

1	2	3	4	5	6	7	8	9	10	11	12	13
14	15	16	17	18	19	20	21	22	23	24	25	26

Codeword 11

22	15	22	15	18 **L**	16	■	21	■	4	13	5	
■	11	■	13	■	2	■	25	3	24	11	■	16
11	6	16	26	18	13	10	■	16	■	11	24	16
■	16	■	■	16	■	3	10	7	■	■	22	■
10	26	11	2	16	22	9	■	2	16	17	2	7
13	■	13	■	26	■	1	■	■	5	■	2	■
20 **R**	16	20	3	7	16	■	10	23	11	2	11	7
■	13	■	7	■	■	23	■	13	■	8	■	3
5	26	22	16	20	■	3	9	22	20	11	26	19
■	2	■	■	13 **A**	10	16	■	26	■	■	16	■
8	23	12	■	3	■	7	11	12	14	16	13	9
20	■	22	24	18	16	■	9	■	22	■	24	■
12	16	9	■	2	■	■	16	19	14	26	12	11

A B C D E F G H I J K L M
N O P Q R S T U V W X Y Z

1	2	3	4	5	6	7	8	9	10	11	12	13
14	15	16	17	18	19	20	21	22	23	24	25	26

Codeword 12

13		9		18		26		13		14		14
23	6	8	26	2	23	19		8	3	22	16	23
15		16		16		22		7		2		15
5	8	10	22	16		20	2	7	12	16	22	24
8		6		8				19				19
	26	14	23	16	23	26	25 T	22	16	2	17	22
13		8				8				15		6
22	11	3	19	8	2	25	23	25	2 I	21	22	
24				13				23		23		13
16	22 E	1	12	22	6	25		16	8	24	22	8
8		12		4		2		2		2		8
8	21	23	25	22		24	22	20	2	15	22	6
18		4		24		22		20		7		25

A B C D E F G H I J K L M
N O P Q R S T U V W X Y Z

| 1 | 2 | 3 | 4 | 5 | 6 | 7 | 8 | 9 | 10 | 11 | 12 | 13 |
| 14 | 15 | 16 | 17 | 18 | 19 | 20 | 21 | 22 | 23 | 24 | 25 | 26 |

Codeword 13

	24		24		1 **N**		12		4		10
	4	11	1	11	4	12		3	8	12	6	2
	21		1		22	1	8		11		21
7	12	19	19	21	18			12	22	18	25	17
15			13			13		12		17	
21	1	24	25	4	7		12	19	10 **S**	25	1
10		12			19	21	9			9		21
	14	8	16	22	21 **E**		21	20	5	12	1	16
	12		21		17				11		11
16	19	12	17	1			10	8	1	10	21	24
12		13		25	19	7		18		18	
23	19	25	26	21		19	12	1	22	21	16
24		15		10		25		12		17	

A	B	C	D	E	F	G	H	I	J	K	L	M
N	O	P	Q	R	S	T	U	V	W	X	Y	Z

1	2	3	4	5	6	7	8	9	10	11	12	13
14	15	16	17	18	19	20	21	22	23	24	25	26

18		16		19				18		6 **O**		9
7	2	7	1	23	12	7		7	18	18	6	18
10		11		5		5		1		8		6
25	23	12		17	18	6	3	6	20	10 **I**	25	9
8				7		12		23		25		
7	8	9	7	8		10	5	17 **P**	7	24	1	15
7		7				6				18		23
18	23	25	8	6	4	25		8	6	13	7	25
		7		18		24		10				8
3	24	18	10	24	21	26	7	11		14	10	18
10		6		26		26		5		23		7
7	22	23	24	26		13	7	24	18	25	7	8
4		11		13				26		20		11

A	B	C	D	E	F	G	H	I	J	K	L	M
N	O	P	Q	R	S	T	U	V	W	X	Y	Z

1	2	3	4	5	6	7	8	9	10	11	12	13
14	15	16	17	18	19	20	21	22	23	24	25	26

Codeword 15

	10	5	16			18	10	26		6	
	23		22	14	1	16		14	5	16	17
9	7	26	14			5	14	11		26	
	15		20	16	1	7		11	14	14	4
21	7	11	2		24			14		4	7	8
10			10	7	20		10	23	9		5	
9	7	14	17		14	23	3		14	23	17	14
	15		1	16	25		3	10	20			20
24	7	17		11			7		22	7	17	10
	17	9	14	25		10	13	23	14		19	
	10		10	7	8			20	16	12	1
	17	2	10	20		8 (M)	7	17	17		7
	14		4	12	16 (O)			14	11 (N)	4

A	B	C	D	E	F	G	H	I	J	K	L	M
N	O	P	Q	R	S	T	U	V	W	X	Y	Z

1	2	3	4	5	6	7	8	9	10	11	12	13
14	15	16	17	18	19	20	21	22	23	24	25	26

Codeword 16

23	18	16	23		6		8		8	1	16	23
4		8		1 L	18	16	20	23		4		11
7	10	8	3		9		15		25	1	11	15
19		11	25	22	9		22	8	13	11		20
	1		21		1	25	2		4		23	
24	4	22	4	11	8		16	15	23	5	18	8
	19			18				25			4	
20	8	1	15	11	25		11	26	18	25	22	11
	23		3		12	25	10		22		9	
15		14	8	26	15		25	4	21	8		8
20 P	8	25	23		25		22 N		15	17	18	16
11		22		21	26	25	19	8		8		4
23	25	2	23		21		23		18	23	8	26

A	B	C	D	E	F	G	H	I	J	K	L	M
N	O	P	Q	R	S	T	U	V	W	X	Y	Z

1	2	3	4	5	6	7	8	9	10	11	12	13
14	15	16	17	18	19	20	21	22	23	24	25	26

Codeword 17

	12		21		13		21		20		22	
20	4	18	20	25	23		6	18	25	6	2	15
	18		5		3	23	2		20		10	
15	20	10	23	5 T	22		20		1	18	6	9
	23				17	4	1				2	
24	4	22	5	23		7		5	22	25	20	2 N
		1		17	23	12	10	20		22		
6	2	1	6	20		18		23	19	6	23	10
	23				11	23	26				2	
23	3	6 I	1		23		13	14	9	6	2	15
	6		20		10	20	6		23		23	
18	20	8	20	17	5		2	22	3	20	10	26
	26		7		16		14		20		26	

A	B	C	D	E	F	G	H	I	J	K	L	M
N	O	P	Q	R	S	T	U	V	W	X	Y	Z

1	2	3	4	5	6	7	8	9	10	11	12	13
14	15	16	17	18	19	20	21	22	23	24	25	26

21		11		6		4		21		16	
1	5	14	26	19	8		24	26	10	20	2	11
3		6		22		18		26		2	
26	11	14	11		23	24	26	3	1	26	6	13
4				8		3		5		24	
2	10 L	5	1	5	17 N	26	4	5	17	15	
13		26					15		1	
2	12	6	2	23	4	5	8	17	26	10
4		5		17		5			25	
23	3	8	1	8	4	2	19	19	3	8	23
22 U		5		2		5		8		3	
16	10	26	7	2	3		2	9	22	26	10	11
13		2		11		11		3		13	

| A | B | C | D | E | F | G | H | I | J | K | L | M |
| N | O | P | Q | R | S | T | U | V | W | X | Y | Z |

1	2	3	4	5	6	7	8	9	10	11	12	13
14	15	16	17	18	19	20	21	22	23	24	25	26

Codeword 19

3	25	25	10	20	1	■	11	15	17	20	17	10
7	■	16 U	■	8	■	16	■	10	■	3	■	14
3	19	19	16	11	17	1	■	12	20	8	13	17
20	■	21	■	17	■	1	■	11	■	5	■	20
■	16	11	17	11	■	17	26	12	10	11	17	11
3	■	8	■	■	■	20	■	8	■	■	■	17
5	17	3 A	20	9	24	■	3	5	2	10	20	3
24	■	■	■	20	■	20	■	■	■	12	■	11
4	17	23	19	10	22	17	■	3	2	3	20	■
21	■	10	■	15	■	12	■	2	■	18	■	8
17	12	10	19	21	■	3	8	20	2	16	5	11
20	■	6	■	17	■	24	■	17	■	17	■	23 L
17	5	11	16	20	17	■	1	17	2	20	17	17

A N B O C P D Q E R F S G T H U I V J W K X L Y M Z

1	2	3	4	5	6	7	8	9	10	11	12	13
14	15	16	17	18	19	20	21	22	23	24	25	26

Codeword 20

	19	9	12 **A**			1	9	23		7	
	3		19	9	16	24		16	9	3	15
13	9	15	24			23	1	9		20	
	16		4	12	23	26		18	6	9	13
21	12	10	17		4			6		23	12	13
6			9	23	24		14	24	7		10	
8	11	4	3		24	19	24		24	12	17	11
	24		15	12	13		10	12	4			12
5	12	25 **D**		19			24		4	12	21	13
	1	3	22	3		13	16	24	12		24	
		2		9	4	24			13	11	4	24
	10	24	16	25		12	15	7	9		9	
	15		17	9	4				15	6	7 **T**	

A	B	C	D	E	F	G	H	I	J	K	L	M
N	O	P	Q	R	S	T	U	V	W	X	Y	Z

1	2	3	4	5	6	7	8	9	10	11	12	13
14	15	16	17	18	19	20	21	22	23	24	25	26

Codeword 21

	4		6		25		3		4		9 **G**
	19	17	13	17	6	5		17	7	20	14	17
		18		5		21	24	6		10		18
13	26	24	5	25	17			5	8	20	25	17
12			13			23		20		5	
23	12	6	15	17	25		17	5	25	14	22
13		5		5	15	5			5		6
	12	25	23	20	6		4	17	4	23	17	25
	1		17		13			5		24
2	14	12	6 **T**	15		20	18	2	12	4	17
5		16		24	25	18		24		11	
13	4	5	14	14		24	18	14	12	5	10 **D**
15		14		14		18		14		22	

A B C D E F G H I J K L M
N O P Q R S T U V W X Y Z

1	2	3	4	5	6	7	8	9	10	11	12	13

14	15	16	17	18	19	20	21	22	23	24	25	26

10		22		22		26		17		13		13
5	21 U	12	3	18	1	23		18	14	18	4	15 R
21		20		10		4		8		25		4
18	12	1	18	14		22	15	18	25	25	8	4
19		24		21				4				18
	14	12	1	10	3	18	3	21	3	18	12	1
10		21				13				1		23
14	18	15	14	21	17	10	3	26	1 N	14	4	
18				1				22		8		14
4	1	6	12	16	4	22		9	12	21	14	7
1		4		12		18		18		22		12
14	8	4	15	11		4	2	14	4	4	22	10
4		15		4		22		4		22		4

A	B	C	D	E	F	G	H	I	J	K	L	M
N	O	P	Q	R	S	T	U	V	W	X	Y	Z

1	2	3	4	5	6	7	8	9	10	11	12	13
14	15	16	17	18	19	20	21	22	23	24	25	26

Codeword 23

3	1	15	22	8	■	4	25	24 **S**	15	1	24	13
■	8	■	2	■	15	■	12	■	14	■	5	■
24	1	6	13	19	17	22	3	■	1	15 **P**	10	24
■	12	■	3	■	1	■	14	■	1	■	22	■
24	13	23	3	13	3	■	1	9	9	13	14	■
■	■	■	13 **E**	■	1	■	4	■	■	■	13	■
11	25	16	4	■	11	12	10	■	2	22	24	21
■	12	■	■	■	14	■	26	■	13	■	■	■
■	18	10	12	3	22	■	3	19	13	16	20	13
■	10	■	1	■	15	■	1	■	24	■	13	■
25	14	1	12	■	17	22	14	4	19	22	14	13
■	13	■	13	■	13	■	7	■	22	■	24	■
13	4	25	3	1	14	24	■	13	23	15	13	16

A B C D E F G H I J K L M
N O P Q R S T U V W X Y Z

1	2	3	4	5	6	7	8	9	10	11	12	13
14	15	16	17	18	19	20	21	22	23	24	25	26

Codeword 24

	11		21		20		13		8		23	
2	26	22	25	20	9		25	7 **P**	25	22	9	15
	10		5		5	18	18		17		26	
14	1	11	18	5	17		13		15	26	22	5
	26				25	7	26				22	
23	18	26	25	14		25		25	3	23	6	17
		3		25	12	15	11	11		25		
25	3	3	6	24		26		4	5	18	18	11
	25			3	26	16				6		
23	17	25	22		26		18	5	17	26	25	3
	23		26		18	26	5		25		2	
9	26	3	17	5	25		17	6	5	11	26	11
	2		22 **T**		19		23		18		2	

A	B	C	D	E	F	G	H	I	J	K	L	M
N	O	P	Q	R	S	T	U	V	W	X	Y	Z

1	2	3	4	5	6	7	8	9	10	11	12	13
14	15	16	17	18	19	20	21	22	23	24	25	26

Codeword 25

	6	20	5	9 (O)	3	12	26		2	20	18	22
11		17		23		17		11		21		2
14	9	17	7	26	10	22		17	9	11	22	26
11		12		5		12		20		20		8
18	12	21	11	1		5	20	5	26	22	18	
20				9		26		18		26		6
18	2	5	9	25	17 (N)		18	11	22	22	12	26
26		26		26		22		19				16
	15	21	9	5	26	18		12 (U)	17	19	21	26
20		20		11		20		21		5		25
23	11	13	26	17		5	26	20	21	11	24	26
26		26		4		18		18		26		21
5	26	8	9		20	22	19	26	17	8	22	

A B C D E F G H I J K L M
N O P Q R S T U V W X Y Z

1	2	3	4	5	6	7	8	9	10	11	12	13
								O				

14	15	16	17	18	19	20	21	22	23	24	25	26
			N									

Codeword 26

4	1	24	20		12		22		13	17	1	13
13		7		23	15	6	5	2		1		7
21	4	16	8		6		8		24	15	4	20
10		1	2	6	13		16	4	15	24		4
	25		1		3	1	24		3		15	
8	3	1	4	18	5		20	14	20	9	24	21
	15			13				13			9	
13	2	10	13	2	15		12	3 **R**	15	8	7	24
	2		19		4	16	13		25		5	
9		24	13	4	18		25	5	20	25		18 **P**
16	12	20	5		13		8		21	1	4	16
1		11		23	15	25 **D**	20	16		26		1
18	15	24	5		3		3		13	26	13	3

A B C D E F G H I J K L M
N O P Q R S T U V W X Y Z

1	2	3	4	5	6	7	8	9	10	11	12	13
14	15	16	17	18	19	20	21	22	23	24	25	26

Codeword 27

20	11	9	19	1	4	12		12	11	19	12	10
	19		24		13		12		26		10	
14	7	19	6	20	21 T	19	21	20	26	2	19	1
	7		4		7		19				9	
18	26	15 U	7	2	19	1	12		23	4	4	3
	17		12				20		7		12	
	7	4	25	15	4	12	21	4	24			
	23		1		9				19		15	
9	7	4	16		24	7	20	2	22	20	2	14
	26				19		2		24		3	
20	2	12	21	20	21	15	21	20	26	2	19	1 L
	5		26		4		7		17		20	
23	4	7	16	1		8	26	7	2	4	7	12

A B C D E F G H I J K L M
N O P Q R S T U V W X Y Z

1	2	3	4	5	6	7	8	9	10	11	12	13
14	15	16	17	18	19	20	21	22	23	24	25	26

Codeword 28

	8	26	21			24	9	12		20	
	24		17	19	24	9		10	9	15	4
13	26	21	17			9	12	14		24	
	25		11 (P)	12	10	5 (S)		15	5	24	10
5	23	12	23		7			5		8	12	2
26			17	10	24		24	6	12		22	
5	17	15	21		24	17	8		25	23	24	24
	8		24	2	2		24	12	9			21
26	1	24		24			4 (M)		24	16	12	4
	24	19	26	21		21	3	9	24		21	
		24		26	9	24			26	1	17	8
	18	9	24	24		24	21	12	8		15	
		3		18	26	9			25	17	10	

A B C D E F G H I J K L M
N O P Q R S T U V W X Y Z

1	2	3	4	5	6	7	8	9	10	11	12	13
14	15	16	17	18	19	20	21	22	23	24	25	26

Codeword 29

	13		16		10			24		2		4 R
19	9	23	2	16	4			1	4	16	24	1	21
	24		5		18 U		18		24		13	
21	15	1	15		2	5	21	20	5	3	16	21
	16				10		16		7		21	
16	26	1	10	10	16	4	1	15	16	21		
	15 T		4					24		13		
	19	1	4	15	24	16	4	21	11	5	19
	13		15		11		24			4	
14	18	5	16	15	16	21	15		17	9	13	3
	15		22		9		9		5		20	
20	5	14	18	9	4		6	9	25	5	16	21
	16		20		12		8		16		21	

A	B	C	D	E	F	G	H	I	J	K	L	M
N	O	P	Q	R	S	T	U	V	W	X	Y	Z

1	2	3	4	5	6	7	8	9	10	11	12	13
14	15	16	17	18	19	20	21	22	23	24	25	26

Codeword 30

A	B	C	D	E	F	G	H	I	J	K	L	M
N	O	P	Q	R	S	T	U	V	W	X	Y	Z

1	2	3	4	5	6	7	8	9	10	11	12	13
14	15	16	17	18	19	20	21	22	23	24	25	26

Grid clues (11 = I, 16 = D, 19 = S):

15		3		4		10		21		23		10
19	6	15	6	11	24	25		15	24	24	10	9
13		13		22		25		25		10		13
11 (I)	20	13	10	22		19	18	1	10	10	8	10
26		11		10				15				24
	3	10	15	16	18	1	15	7	6	10	7	19
16 (D)		19				19				15		10
11	24	6	10	7	20	10	16	11	15	6	10	
19				10				24		15		12
10	2	10	14	15	22	22		19	17	14	10	7
15		4		22		17		1		22		11
19 (S)	6	10	10	22		14	10	22	11	10	5	10
10		7		2		19		6		19		19

Codeword 31

	19		9		7		5		21		2	
3	16	24	2	11	19		21	4	11	2	1	17
	2		20		13	15	17		17		2	
20	13	17	17 E	12	17		13		11	19	6	10
	1				10	13 R	15				7	
26	6	7	7	6		16		22	13	6 O	11	11
		16		25	16	20	26	17		16		
22	13	21	25	25		20		24	16	23	17	1
	17				3	2	1				24	
2	11	26	17		6		16	20	26	16	12	17
	17		8		7	6	13		6		15	
16	7	7	2	13	17		17	24	18	16	14	4
	11		7		13		1		6		17	

A B C D E F G H I J K L M
N O P Q R S T U V W X Y Z

1	2	3	4	5	6	7	8	9	10	11	12	13
14	15	16	17	18	19	20	21	22	23	24	25	26

Codeword 32

	13		8		10		14		12		16
8	11	11	14	16	25		10	14	25	16	22
	25		11		15	12	21		11		23
22	19	15	4	16	25			2	10	13	7	11
11			11			17		15		10	
2	10	15	19	13	23 **G**		11	5	6	16	22
16		12		12	22	13			22		10
	25	16	9	10	3		16	1	5	22	10	15 **S**
	12 **U**		12		15				11		24
26	11	18	16	14			10	14	18	10	3	15
10		19		12	24	15		11		13	
15	10	8	16	15		16	20	12	10	5	16
5		16		6		5		25		15	

A B C D E F G H I J K L M
N O P Q R S T U V W X Y Z

1	2	3	4	5	6	7	8	9	10	11	12	13
14	15	16	17	18	19	20	21	22	23	24	25	26

Codeword 33

	9		10	13	10	1	26	18	2		26	
22	26	9	15		25		23		17	5	5	18
	8		11	24	7	22	17	10	22 **R**		18	
1	17	18	2		26		24		10	19	24	18
	8			15	26	16	10		24		5
20	17	5	10		24				18	24	21	26
10		24	3	10	22	5	24	24	4	18		18
15	7	6	10			7 **U**		13	10	26	2
10		6		18	5	24	15			16	
21 **D**	26	13	18		26		18	9	10	26	4
	22		2	24	18	15	17	5	10		12	
16	17	8	17		18		21		5	10	10	18
	26		9	22	24	14	10	11	15		18	

A B C D E F G H I J K L M
N O P Q R S T U V W X Y Z

1	2	3	4	5	6	7	8	9	10	11	12	13
14	15	16	17	18	19	20	21	22	23	24	25	26

Codeword 34

14	1	26	16	14	24		12	24	22	11	4	9
	26 U		2		10		21		21		16	
24	10	5	24		21	19	21	15	24	16	9	12
	12		10		22				16		12	
15	21	14	21	12	16		3	16	6	22	10	2
			23		22		10				9	
18	21	18	21	2	16	9		13	26	5	14	
	8				24		16		16			
14	15	11	11	20	25		19	26	18	6	16	22
	21		11				10		18		17	
14	2	24	18	16	19	12	7		10	17	11	19
	12		15		21		21		9 N		15	
16	14	12	24	18	16		14 S	10	5	24	12	14

A	B	C	D	E	F	G	H	I	J	K	L	M
N	O	P	Q	R	S	T	U	V	W	X	Y	Z

1	2	3	4	5	6	7	8	9	10	11	12	13

14	15	16	17	18	19	20	21	22	23	24	25	26

Codeword 35

7	18	3	9	7	7			19		3	14	4
	11		4		14		19	9	18	20		20
3	9	15	12	9	7	18		25		1	20	26
	18			6		20	16	25			4	
4	20	14	25	6	8	21		20	3	3	20	26
12		25		9		14			9		10	
4	9	25	8	23	26		2	8	19	19	9	9
	20		23			22		19		20		16
20	7	22	9	23 **D**		20	19	19	20	6	25	9
	9			3	9	24		20			14	
9	25	22		26		20	5 **P**	25	9	17 **N**	18	26
8		9	3	20	7		20		9		11	
17	20	13		23		16	20	25	25	9	18

A B C D E F G H I J K L M
N O P Q R S T U V W X Y Z

1	2	3	4	5	6	7	8	9	10	11	12	13
14	15	16	17	18	19	20	21	22	23	24	25	26

20	4	19	16		7		8		18	7	23	8
25		26		19	20	26	18	19		23		26
12	18	11	18		4		21		15	20	23	6
16		25 **I**	21	5	4		19	26	18	20		8
	22		8		19	3	26		20		7	
9	4	19	25	5	3		9	4	16	10	23	26
	25			26				14			16	
23	16	18	12	26 **E**	16		18	11	25	12	24	8
	8		18		18	20	15		19		3	
16		18	13	25	19		15	18	11	5		18
11	4	7	26		19		26		3	18	14	16
18		26		8	26	9	17	8		1		2
17	18	8	24		21 **N**		8		11	26	16	16

A	B	C	D	E	F	G	H	I	J	K	L	M
N	O	P	Q	R	S	T	U	V	W	X	Y	Z

1	2	3	4	5	6	7	8	9	10	11	12	13
14	15	16	17	18	19	20	21	22	23	24	25	26

Codeword 37

	21		15		6		21		12		13
	18	22	8	22	2	22		16	20	14	9	15
		2		9		4	14	24		2		16
16	2	4	25	24	16			25	19	9	12 **T**	16
4			22				11		22		9	
23	25 **O**	15	15	25	1		25	7	7 **D**	16	24	
25		16			22	2	8			12		6
	17	22	2	12	10		16	10	4	9	17	16
	24		9		16				25			6
23	25	18	18	5			12	14	3	16	7	25
25		5		14	17	10		24		13		
25	17	12	22	4		16	2	13	9	13	16	
26		16		8		1		16		5		

A B C D E F G H I J K L M
N O P Q R S T U V W X Y Z

1	2	3	4	5	6	7	8	9	10	11	12	13
14	15	16	17	18	19	20	21	22	23	24	25	26

Codeword 38

	11	22	7	8	15	9	3		2	11	5	19
1		20		5		21		19		4		5
5	24	8	21	19 R	4	11		5	10	7	4	5
14		5		11		22		22		19		26
11	4	19	15	8		5	24	7	10	4	11	
15				5		11		14		10		13
4	21	8	15	23	11		23	15	9	5	13	7
5		15		4		7		10				5
	5	4	22	15	23	11		15	21	4	7	11
25		12		17		22		4		19		4
5	17	7	6	5		21	8	7	18	2 U	5	19
11		10		11		19		4		11		21 O
4	7	10	5		19	5	16	5	23	4	11	

A	B	C	D	E	F	G	H	I	J	K	L	M
N	O	P	Q	R	S	T	U	V	W	X	Y	Z

1	2	3	4	5	6	7	8	9	10	11	12	13
14	15	16	17	18	19	20	21	22	23	24	25	26

Codeword 39

	4	15	13	14	23	21	2		24	26	26	2
4		23		2		4			6		11	
9	25	6	19	26		23	14	20	26	23	6	21
6		5		4		26 E		14			4	
2	14	21	24		2	26	22	18	26	4	3 T	4
3		15		13		17		25		18		
	4	3	14	18	3		21	24	14	20	26	
		6		5		18		4		4		18
25	26	15	9	20	21	25	24		1	6	16	4
	21			18		6		23		24		21
20	2	14	18	16	13	3		14	12	6	25 N	16
	23		4			26		15		7		26
3	8	17	26		21	24	10	6	4	26	4	

A	B	C	D	E	F	G	H	I	J	K	L	M
N	O	P	Q	R	S	T	U	V	W	X	Y	Z

1	2	3	4	5	6	7	8	9	10	11	12	13
14	15	16	17	18	19	20	21	22	23	24	25	26

Codeword 40

22	15	5	13	16	7 **I**		24	7	24	10	26	10
	13		7		18		10		8		7	
14	15	12	12 **T**		10	14	14	8	25	21	5	26
	10		15		4				1		6	
10	16	23	10	16	7		13	11	18	12	10	20
			12		16		14				8	
22	5	3	5		7	8	5		22	25	26	5
	2				12		24		10			
6	15	17	5	16	11		7	18	19	5 **E**	24	12
	10		16				9		25		10	
17	16	10	26	7	25	16	7		8	7	4	13
	16		5		16		5		16		7	
6	11	4	8	7	26		13	10	11	7	18	17

A	B	C	D	E	F	G	H	I	J	K	L	M
N	O	P	Q	R	S	T	U	V	W	X	Y	Z

1	2	3	4	5	6	7	8	9	10	11	12	13
14	15	16	17	18	19	20	21	22	23	24	25	26

Codeword 41

7	24	9	6	■	18	■	4	■	10	23	18	21
1	■	26	■	14	13	1	26	17	■	18	■	10
14	26	14	12	■	1 (U)	■	6	■	23	18	15	2 (N)
23	■	11	26	11	26	■	10	4	24	2	■	19
■	16	■	6	■	6	24	11	■	1	■	5	■
5	6	24	24	17	14	■	12	26	15	17	6	25
■	26	■	■	1	■	■	■	14	■	■	18	■
26	8	26	6	18	26	■	4	12	24	14	18	2
■	18	■	24	■	20	10	24	■	3	■	23	■
14	■	9	26	17	10	■	15	18	18	5	■	26
4	25	26	2	■	17	■	15	■	15	10	24	23
1	■	15	■	15	18	6	26	22	■	14	■	24
17	1	17 (D)	14	■	14	■	6	■	14	23	18	21

A B C D E F G H I J K L M
N O P Q R S T U V W X Y Z

1	2	3	4	5	6	7	8	9	10	11	12	13

14	15	16	17	18	19	20	21	22	23	24	25	26

Grid clues (with given letters: 26 = U, 11 = G, 21 = M):

	7		2		10		7		6		15
	13	1	9	8	24	13		5	26	8	12	17
		3		13		13	21	26 (U)		24		8
13	19	13	12	23	15			7	25	20	15	15
3			18			12		7		8	
21	7	15	15	8	10		26	23	23	13	24
15		14			18	7	23			18		7
	23	20	8	4	11 (G)		13	22	13	4	13	2
	6		12		15				25			2
4	18	23	13	2			24	18	25	18	23	15
7		24		18	24	12		26		8	
25	3	8	23	16		7	25	15	13	4	23
15		21 (M)		13		20		23		17

A B C D E F G H I J K L M
N O P Q R S T U V W X Y Z

1	2	3	4	5	6	7	8	9	10	11	12	13
14	15	16	17	18	19	20	21	22	23	24	25	26

Codeword 43

	5		11		9		12		1		25	
26 **S**	24	16	24	5	22		16	22	3	24	13	6 **D**
	20		1		25	14	24		24		14	
4	24	1	7	16	14		5		13	22	12	12
	17				6	15	14				22	
20	14	22	17	18		24		25	13	23	21	15
		16		23	4	18	14	13		8		
18	24	16	8	14		23		15	14	24	13	20
	5			10	23	24				24	
14	25	22	1		22		1	23	23	7	22	14
	16		23		10	24	18		5		26	
26	14	19	2	14	16		14	21	22	4	14	6
	13		25		14 **E**		26		4		26	

A	B	C	D	E	F	G	H	I	J	K	L	M
N	O	P	Q	R	S	T	U	V	W	X	Y	Z

1	2	3	4	5	6	7	8	9	10	11	12	13
14	15	16	17	18	19	20	21	22	23	24	25	26

	10	25	25	10	15	3	4		20	5	7	4
22		15		3		10			22		10	
12	22	24	19	6		23	19 **O**	24	7	22	14	7
15		15		8		15		10			15	
26	5	4	7		26	10	9	15	24	22	4	4
4		18		1		26		26		16		
	7	15	7	10	24		6	22	24	5	4	
		24		26		4		17		15		10
5 **U**	3	13	22	24	7	26	8		4	21	10	24
	19			5		15		10		6		2
10	11	22	7	7	22	17		11	22	22	23	18
	19		10			22		26		24		4
10	7	19	21		10	4	4	22	3 **R**	7	4	

```
A   B   C   D   E   F   G   H   I   J   K   L   M
N   O   P   Q   R   S   T   U   V   W   X   Y   Z
```

1	2	3	4	5	6	7	8	9	10	11	12	13
14	15	16	17	18	19	20	21	22	23	24	25	26

	7	11	18	4	2	17	21		23	18	11	15
12		7		14		20				2		2
17	20	7	8 (L)	20	18	4		24	16	16	20	17
11		24		17		6		16		4		16
25	24	1	24	20		17	20	12	24	2	16	
14			11		16		17		17			26
24	15	22	24 (I)	22	20		4	11	4	4	2	2
18		17		2 (O)		11		4				6
	9	11	18	6	6	15		24	16	4	20	17
23		18		4		6		4		19		16
4	11	3	20	23		23	13	6	20	20	5	20
11		20				20		10		20		21
22	20	4	23		11	23	18	20	16	10	23	

A	B	C	D	E	F	G	H	I	J	K	L	M
N	O	P	Q	R	S	T	U	V	W	X	Y	Z

1	2	3	4	5	6	7	8	9	10	11	12	13
14	15	16	17	18	19	20	21	22	23	24	25	26

Codeword 46

	7		6		23		22		22		20	
11	1	6	19	11	1		8	26	14	26	1	22
	8		15		8		10		19		16 G	
9	1	25	26		8	26	4	26	8	11	26	3
	3				26		10		1		11	
21	19	5	11	12	15	22	1	5	21	2		
	17		22						10		3	
	9	8	26	18	12	26	5	21	10	26	11	
	26		26		12		5				21	
26	4	1	11 S	10	19	5	11		6	10	15	13
	10		11		22		12		19 O		1	
11	21	14	26	6	26		8	26	24	19	10	5
	22		11		3		26		19		6	

A	B	C	D	E	F	G	H	I	J	K	L	M
N	O	P	Q	R	S	T	U	V	W	X	Y	Z

1	2	3	4	5	6	7	8	9	10	11	12	13
14	15	16	17	18	19	20	21	22	23	24	25	26

Codeword 47

	17		9 T		23		21		25		19
24	19	24	17	2	16		22	19	4	25	22
	6		18		11	17	17		25		14
12	17	1	18	3	6		21	17	2	9	2
16			16			26		16		16 A	
20	16	24 M	20	17	17		19	13	18	25	22
2		16		13	19	23			16		7
	16	23	9	6	1		2	3	20	9	6	1
	2		17		8			19			24
9	7	17	22	13		16	9	9	16	19	13
17		20		19	13	14		7		2	
11	22	17	13	5		25	10	3	19	23	2
13		25		7		5		15		2	

A B C D E F G H I J K L M
N O P Q R S T U V W X Y Z

1	2	3	4	5	6	7	8	9	10	11	12	13

14	15	16	17	18	19	20	21	22	23	24	25	26

Codeword 48

		15		8		20		16		16	
8	10	10	14	1		8	9	10	15	10	21
4		25		15		12		15		4		15
14	19 P	15	12	26	18	14		22	13	26	9	10
24		21		18		4 D		26				20
16	13	10	8		26		7	23	14	14	3	14
8		15		21 G	13	14	8	18		6		23
12	23	8	4	14	4		23		23	15	2	14
14				10		16		8		4		10
13	14	8	6	14		25	16	7	17	14	2	12
5		15		23		15		14		10		13
	26	23	4	8	15	10		12	8	2	11	5
		5		13		21		25		14		

A	B	C	D	E	F	G	H	I	J	K	L	M
N	O	P	Q	R	S	T	U	V	W	X	Y	Z

1	2	3	4	5	6	7	8	9	10	11	12	13
14	15	16	17	18	19	20	21	22	23	24	25	26

Codeword 49

17	9	12	26	15	23		22	1	14	10	22	25
11		10		4		2		14		2		9
4	19	8	14	22	24	4	17	26		2	14	19
12 **M**		9		10		19		22		5		26
10	4	5		6	10	17	10	24	4	9	19	22
18				9		25				19		24
	22	13	10	20	19		12	10	24	24	26	
2		10				22		13				26
4	19	15	4	17	10	24	9	5		22	9	19
22		15		10		10		4		10		7
17	25	4		3	10 **A**	22	4	17	10	11	11	23
10		19		4		25			9		6		12
11	26	21 **G**	26	19	15		22	24	5	9	16	26

| A | B | C | D | E | F | G | H | I | J | K | L | M |
| N | O | P | Q | R | S | T | U | V | W | X | Y | Z |

1	2	3	4	5	6	7	8	9	10	11	12	13
14	15	16	17	18	10	20	21	22	23	24	25	26

Codeword 50

	7		24		2		16		24		25	
19	23	10	3 (P)	25	26		15	7	19	25	20	14
	4		10		18	4	25		25		13 (D)	
13	23	8	25	20	10		7		10	6	18	9
	4				10	14	21				20	
4	23	7	19	18		23		24	13	24	19	25
		25		22	23	6	25	26		7		
1	25	12	14	21		25		26	18	11	25	13
	10				25	26	12				7	
10	4	24	7		20		18	20	5	15	7	25
	24		15 (U)		14	24	17		25		24	
10	3	18	13	25	7		25	17	14	24	20	14
	25		13		21		13		10		13	

A	B	C	D	E	F	G	H	I	J	K	L	M
N	O	P	Q	R	S	T	U	V	W	X	Y	Z

1	2	3 P	4	5	6	7	8	9	10	11	12	13 D
14	15 U	16	17	18	19	20	21	22	23	24	25	26

10	15	7	12	14	15			12		14	19	10
	7		15		15		23	2	24	15		21 **A**
19	18	19	21	14	14	22		20		3	6	18
	19			22		15	12	21			2	
11	15	20	14	3	5	21		1	15	4	11	21
2		15		7		17			10		8	
15	7	11	21	10	15		10	14	2	18	18	22
	21		5			18		2		24		15
8	3	14	15	18		12	2 **O**	21	16 **D**	3	15	18
	13			20	11	2		16			26	
11	15	16		15		9	21	18	17	12	19	4
3		3	8	21	8		22			3		3
4	2	20		24			15	25	5	15	20	12

| A | B | C | D | E | F | G | H | I | J | K | L | M |
| N | O | P | Q | R | S | T | U | V | W | X | Y | Z |

1	2	3	4	5	6	7	8	9	10	11	12	13
14	15	16	17	18	19	20	21	22	23	24	25	26

A B C D E F G H I J K L M
N O P Q R S T U V W X Y Z

1	2	3	4	5	6	7	8	9	10	11	12	13
14	15	16	17	18	19	20	21	22	23	24	25	26

4	17	23	8		14		19		4	6	17	4
16		4 **P**		15	10	26	17	13		10		17
23	7	16	19		2		21		18	16	22	17
23		22	17	13	11		10	1	3	14		14
	25		16		3	24	13		7		18	
25	16	21	11	16	6		23	9	10	14	14	23
	12		14				3 **O**			10		
16	12	16	14	17	16		18	10	23	5	17	1
	20		10		4	5	10		16		23	
4		17	15	10	14		1	17	24	20		24
14	20	6 **R**	17		3		21		23	17	22	10
3		16		11	22	19	17	6		14		22
4	3	23	17		19		8		23	14	10	4

A	B	C	D	E	F	G	H	I	J	K	L	M
N	O	P	Q	R	S	T	U	V	W	X	Y	Z

1	2	3	4	5	6	7	8	9	10	11	12	13
14	15	16	17	18	19	20	21	22	23	24	25	26

18	24	17	25	19	22		5	7	8	18 **R**	26	19
24		18		13		8		11		8		6
15	24	8	3	23	26	12		8	3	23	7	25
7		1		21		8		21		15		7
	24	8	9	19		23	21	4 **P**	8	19	19	7
10		3				26		15 **L**				14
23	18	24	26	7	3		19	7	3	8	22	7
12				2		8				20		3
16	8	18	3	7	26	19		12	18	8	17	
22		24		20		23		8		3		19
23	26	12	24	22		3	8	21	4	7	19	22
26		25		7		7		25		21		25
12	18	7	7	3	5		19	22	8	5	7	3

A B C D E F G H I J K L M
N O P Q R S T U V W X Y Z

| 1 | 2 | 3 | 4 | 5 | 6 | 7 | 8 | 9 | 10 | 11 | 12 | 13 |
| 14 | 15 | 16 | 17 | 18 | 19 | 20 | 21 | 22 | 23 | 24 | 25 | 26 |

	23	9	7	13	24	23	22	■	12	7	1	9
17		7	■	7	■	9	■	■	11	■	■	11
23	11	22	19	14	5	16	■	23	26	23	2	19
13	■	23	■	5	■	22	■	20	■	6	■	18 **D**
23	24	12	19	12	■	20	14	5	12	20	19	■
14 **N**	■	■	■	24	■	26	■	7	■	19	■	12
13	22	24	26	1	9	■	19	26	19	12	21	19
16	■	14	■	20	■	5	■	7	■	■	■	17
	23	17	23	5	23	12	■	1	12	23	10	19
23		7	■	7	■	24	■	24	■	22	■	12
4	7	10	19	12	■	25	19	22	22	7	3	9 **S**
23	■	19	■	■	■	22	■	19	■	15	■	19
12	23	9	11	■	1	19	19	9	3	23	8	■

A	B	C	D	E	F	G	H	I	J	K	L	M
N	O	P	Q	R	S	T	U	V	W	X	Y	Z

1	2	3	4	5	6	7	8	9	10	11	12	13
14	15	16	17	18	19	20	21	22	23	24	25	26

Codeword 56

	16		19		14		8		9		26
22	19	4	7	15	1		2	4	2	20	5
	14		19		26	15	5		26		19
15	8	8	2	4	26			19	7	15	1	25
17			5				11		1		14
2	18	9	19	1	10		2 E	23	3	19	6
1		15			19	14	10 D			14		21
	19	9	9	6	25		26	12	2	6	17	2
	26		2		26				6			5
20	12	14	20	13			2	8	8	19	20	2
15		10		14	21	9 P		6		25	
11	2	6	15	16			19	21	19	24	2	10
26		2		14		9		1		26	

| A | B | C | D | E | F | G | H | I | J | K | L | M |
| N | O | P | Q | R | S | T | U | V | W | X | Y | Z |

1	2	3	4	5	6	7	8	9	10	11	12	13
14	15	16	17	18	19	20	21	22	23	24	25	26

Codeword 57

Grid (numbers shown; ■ = blocked cell; given letters noted):

	14	■	4	■	25	■	18	■	19	■	3	
3	10	14	25	7	4	■	7	15	21	14	10	23
■	11	■	17	■	4	■	19	■	6	■	10	
23	8	12	5	■	8	15	6	10	16	16 (T)	12	10
■	7	■	■	■	14	■	4	■	14	■	6	
4	14	19	18	16	6	13	25	24	19	15	■	
■	10	■	25	■	■	■	■	■	4	■	10	
	17	14	25	6	17	10	4	16	7	2	10	
■	16	■	10	■	10	■	19	■	■	10		
5	19	4	3	16	7	15	9 (G)	■	26	8	15	1
	20	■	10	■	22	■	12	■	8	■	7	
23	10	4	19	23	10	■	10	14	24	7	15 (N)	10
■	6	■	23	■	23	■	6	■	17	■	9	

Letter key:

A B C D E F G H I J K L M
N O P Q R S T U V W X Y Z

1	2	3	4	5	6	7	8	9	10	11	12	13

14	15	16	17	18	19	20	21	22	23	24	25	26

Codeword 58

	3		16	15	24	23	20	24	14		19	
1	6	5	9		22		7		15	2	15 **I**	24
	14		4	11	20	14	15	9	7		7	
14	5	6	10		6		9		24	14	6	13
	15				6	9	7	24		17		15
6	4	17	9		1				16	15	6	16
21		11	18	14	6	5	7	9	9 **O**	7		9
25	20	14	14				6		24	10	6	13
6		6		6	16	23	6				26	
12	11	16	8		13		16		24	6	6	24
	14		9	19	6	5	12	11	25		4	
3	9	9	5		6		6		5	9	14	6
	25		6	3	2	11 **A**	24	24	8		24	

```
A   B   C   D   E   F   G   H   I   J   K   L   M
N   O   P   Q   R   S   T   U   V   W   X   Y   Z
```

1	2	3	4	5	6	7	8	9	10	11	12	13
14	15	16	17	18	19	20	21	22	23	24	25	26

Codeword 59

7	11	13	24	13	7		7	26	14	24	13	7
24		10		5		20		14		13		25
11	14	23	23	24	5	10	1	7		13	8	2
10		10		10		11		7		7		8
21	8	20		21	10	19	16	21 **N**	24	23	7	11
18				7		8				2 **P**		7
	24	9	8	5	13		24	18 **G**	24	13	7	
7		24				24		21				7
23	24	21	10	22	7	11	13	8		12	24	5
9		24		3		11		19		14		24
5	14	21		8	4	7	5	19	8	23	7	11
6		24		15		13		17		2		7
8	9	11	7	11	11		9	10	24	11	7	20

A	B	C	D	E	F	G	H	I	J	K	L	M
N	O	P	Q	R	S	T	U	V	W	X	Y	Z

1	2	3	4	5	6	7	8	9	10	11	12	13
14	15	16	17	18	19	20	21	22	23	24	25	26

Codeword 60

Given letters: **P** = 3, **M** = 9, **O** = 21

A	B	C	D	E	F	G	H	I	J	K	L	M
N	O	P	Q	R	S	T	U	V	W	X	Y	Z

1	2	3	4	5	6	7	8	9	10	11	12	13
14	15	16	17	18	19	20	21	22	23	24	25	26

Codeword 61

	24	17	21	3	23	22	26		23	16	17	21
9		7		24		23			21		7	
1	6	17	23	10		18	25	8	26	7	1	26
23		1		26		23		13			26	
18	24	17	21		26	15	13	23 (A)	17	1	21	1
2		23		11		19		1		24		
	11	18	17 (U)	25	10 (D)		21	26	3	2	1	
		18		18		23		1		26		22
20	24	19	1	21	25	8	4		26	5	26	3
	3			26		8		14		13		24
24	16	1	26	3	12	26		25	10	26	23	1
	25		23			1		7		3		1
1	21	25	3		9	1	19	8	13	26	10	

A	B	C	D	E	F	G	H	I	J	K	L	M
N	O	P	Q	R	S	T	U	V	W	X	Y	Z

1	2	3	4	5	6	7	8	9	10	11	12	13
14	15	16	17	18	19	20	21	22	23	24	25	26

Codeword 62

	17		11		5		17		22		20	
24	3	11	13	3	1		15	26	3	8	15	4
	10		5		5		23		18		26	
23	5	2	21		17	13	25	24	3	22	24	21
	14				4		3		24		7	
22	15	5	10	3	20	16	5	4	3	22		
	5		26						6		4	
	3	14	4	26	10	17	10	26	4 **T**	26	10	
	9		26		5		23				14	
2	26	21	12	23 **O**	10	1 **D**	20		7	3	20	4
	26		3		14		3		24		3	
17	10	3	14	22	26		14	26	13	10	23	14
	20		8		1		8		19		14	

A	B	C	D	E	F	G	H	I	J	K	L	M
N	O	P	Q	R	S	T	U	V	W	X	Y	Z

1	2	3	4	5	6	7	8	9	10	11	12	13
14	15	16	17	18	19	20	21	22	23	24	25	26

Codeword 63

	20		9		7		25		4		11
	10	14	7	14	16	23		20	14	23	19	22
	18		23		15	13	22		8		23
21	14	7	7	18	17			21	18 **L**	23	24	6
14			23				12		17		2	
20	2	21	13	2	21		23	8	23	2	4	
24		26		22	10	17			16 **R**		14	
	21	17	17	7	26		16	23	1	17	16	10
	14		14		10				17			20
5	16	23	24	17		18	22	3	22	16	26
23		16		15	2	8		15		16	
8	2	23 **I**	13	15		2	13	18	23	13	17
17		10		26		15		26		10	

A	B	C	D	E	F	G	H	I	J	K	L	M
N	O	P	Q	R	S	T	U	V	W	X	Y	Z

1	2	3	4	5	6	7	8	9	10	11	12	13
14	15	16	17	18	19	20	21	22	23	24	25	26

Codeword 64

13	6	7	14	4		18	16	13	17	2	14	7
	7		2		16		21		19		25 **D**	
15	19	21	17	6	10	23	17		23	14	18	6
	23		24		23		6		14		6	
1	6	15	19	10	6		13	14	9	19	13	
		13			13		23				8	
6	7	10 **M**	8		12	16	13		3	6	6	13
	6				6		6		19			
	15	19	10	16	15		17	13	2	21	22	8
	17		6		17 **T**		16		13		21	
5	2	16	17		16	21	18	6	21	17	6	25
	13		6		19		6		6		6	
26	6	14	13	16	21	20		15	11	15	7	6

A B C D E F G H I J K L M
N O P Q R S T U V W X Y Z

1	2	3	4	5	6	7	8	9	10	11	12	13
14	15	16	17	18	19	20	21	22	23	24	25	26

Codeword 65

19	25	10	12	25	12	■	8	12	21	19	12	24
■	10	■	19	■	16 **P**	■	9	■	20	■	10	■
2	4	25 **T**	19	■	5	24	1	20	17	5	10	4
■	12	■	9	■	21	■	■	■	4	■	4	■
19	25	4	10	4	5	■	7	5	10	24	12	21
■	■	4	■	11	■	20	■	■	■	10	■
12	10	20	23	■	20	1	1	■	14	12	19	22
■	4	■	■	13	■	20	■	5	■	■
14	21	20	15	9	4	■	19	9	1	23	10	3
■	4	■	9	■	■	18	■	25	■	20	■
24	12	18	12	10	12	1	20	■	4	23	23 **D**	3
■	19	■	20	■	19	■	1	■	6	■	11	■
26	4	12	21	25	18	■	11	12	25	18	4	10

A	B	C	D	E	F	G	H	I	J	K	L	M
N	O	P	Q	R	S	T	U	V	W	X	Y	Z

1	2	3	4	5	6	7	8	9	10	11	12	13
14	15	16	17	18	19	20	21	22	23	24	25	26

Codeword 66

	8		12		16		16		25		1	
8	25	17	20	16	19		12	20	15	21	14	16
	22		16		16	24	14		22		7	
8	25	18	25	2	3		14		14	10	25	22
	14				14	6	6				15	
13	26	25	21	15		20		11	25	2	14	15
		1		25 I	16	24	22	22		25		
21	5	14	11	21		19		24	14	22	4	15
	25				5	26	3				14	
19	3	7	14		26		22	25	9	20	7	16
	5		24		7 R	5	19		19		15	
7	14	23	14 E	1	21		10	19	19	16	19	19
	7		16		15		14		15		2	

A	B	C	D	E	F	G	H	I	J	K	L	M
N	O	P	Q	R	S	T	U	V	W	X	Y	Z

1	2	3	4	5	6	7	8	9	10	11	12	13
14	15	16	17	18	19	20	21	22	23	24	25	26

Codeword 67

	15		22		23		19		6		5	
18	11	1	20	11	16		23	10	23	19	23	3
	19		2		16		19		5		22	
22	24	23	15		11	13	19	3	23	25	19	22
	12				25		12		3		9	
2	3	23	14	23	19	20	12	15	23	1		
	21		11						17		16	
	7	15	14	11	22	20	3	23	18	1	11	
	25		20		13		15				12	
26	7	4	4	1	20	15	2		26	11	3	21
	3		11		19		11		1		20	
23	10	11	15	7	11		22	8	7	23	22	5
	11		22		14		19		22		19	

| A | B | C | D | E | F | G | H | I | J | K | L | M |
| N | O | P | Q | R | S | T | U | V | W | X | Y | Z |

1	2	3	4	5	6	7	8	9	10	11	12	13
14	15	16	17	18	19	20	21	22	23	24	25	26

17	23	4	14	■	14	■	9	■	25	8	9 **L**	14
25	■	5	■	7	9	25	25	12	■	13	■	1
15	5	26	26	■	23	■	23	■	26	17	25	12
3	■	11	25	5	6	■	26	11	25	13	■	3 **S**
■	18	■	21	■	23	17	14	■	8	■	18 **M**	■
9	23	24	13	25	17	■	17	14	5	3	25	1
■	1	■	■	1	■	■	18	■	■	23	■	■
8	13	23	1	14	5	■	21	13	26	13	17	14
■	3	■	25	■	16	11	23	■	13	■	14	■
5	■	3	13	23	26	■	1	5	7	3	■	5
19	25	23	1	■	23	■	8	■	3	15	5	22
5	■	20	■	9	25	2	14	17	■	13	■	14
17	14	14	10	■	1	■	17	■	23	18	4	3

A B C D E F G H I J K L M
N O P Q R S T U V W X Y Z

1	2	3	4	5	6	7	8	9	10	11	12	13
14	15	16	17	18	19	20	21	22	23	24	25	26

Codeword 69

17	19	14	9	5	■	9	23	16	7	23	17	3
■	10	■	14	■	7	■	21	■	15	■	16	■
13	25	17	3	25	12	19	3	■	22	10	7	9
■	15	■	3	■	15	■	9	■	9	■	23	■
14	22	23	10	25	14	■	14	4	14	20	23	■
■	■	■	23	■	12	■	1	■	■	■	6	■
17	18	23	13	■	14	2	14	■	17	23	23	13
■	14	■	■	■	11	■	11	■	7	■	■	■
■	17	23	25	6	23	■	14	19	9	24	17	17
■	17	■	12 (N)	■	14	■	12	■	1	■	2	■
11 (G)	14	11	14	■	22	14	19	2	23 (E)	10	24	9
■	11	■	12	■	10	■	23	■	8	■	12	■
22	23	26	23	4	23	10	■	14	17	20	23	4

A	B	C	D	E	F	G	H	I	J	K	L	M
N	O	P	Q	R	S	T	U	V	W	X	Y	Z

1	2	3	4	5	6	7	8	9	10	11	12	13
14	15	16	17	18	19	20	21	22	23	24	25	26

23		26		3		25		25		11		15
19	16	1	24	9	18	16		8	13	13	10	25
1		20		20		6		1		10		1
15	22	10	10	1		9	20	10	2	16	24	24
16		19		24				16				7
	5	22	16	25	7	9	13 **O**	20	1	26	24	16
6		15				24				13		19
1	19	7	9	17	22	24	1	7	9	20	23	
20				24				8		16		1
1	15	15	24	9	16	25		16	7	8	9	17
23 **G**		22		6		1		13		16		22
16	4	7	19	1		12	1	19	9	1	20	7
19		25		4		16		21		14 **D**		16

A	B	C	D	E	F	G	H	I	J	K	L	M
N	O	P	Q	R	S	T	U	V	W	X	Y	Z

1	2	3	4	5	6	7	8	9	10	11	12	13
14	15	16	17	18	19	20	21	22	23	24	25	26

	19		17		10		25		14		2
	23	7	22	7	1	7		10	8	7	23	7
		18		18		8	10	15		23		1
16	5	6	5	10	25			7	1	5	6	25
13			5				4		7		10	
6	7	8	8	13	19		5	8	23	13	19	
20		5			5	25	10			16		10
	11	7	12	2	25		8	26	24	23	10	16
	8		26		18				26			5
3	26	7	25	5			11	10	24	13	26	18
26		21		10	24	6		6		26		
10	17	13	19	18		10	17	5	16	18	5	
20		1		5		8		9		25		

U (26) N (1) S (18)

A	B	C	D	E	F	G	H	I	J	K	L	M
N	O	P	Q	R	S	T	U	V	W	X	Y	Z

1	2	3	4	5	6	7	8	9	10	11	12	13
14	15	16	17	18	19	20	21	22	23	24	25	26

Codeword 72

	6	23	19	16	5	14	1		16	19	23	14
6		19		19		9			9		6	
22	6	18	4	14		12	26	19	24	5	8	3
5		18		9		26		26			17	
18	19	19	7		24	9 **E**	10	24	23	19	19	2
9		25		15		16		16		21		
	24	5	6	18 **R**	6		8	6	2	9	7 **D**	
	8		26		6		25		18			13
19	18	3	6	8	5	11	9		6	8	24	5
	6			15		6		24		5		16
6	16	15	19	1	19	16		6	8	3	9	16
	16		16			9		18		1		14
7	20	9	7		15	6	21	19	18	24	14	

A	B	C	D	E	F	G	H	I	J	K	L	M
N	O	P	Q	R	S	T	U	V	W	X	Y	Z

1	2	3	4	5	6	7	8	9	10	11	12	13
14	15	16	17	18	19	20	21	22	23	24	25	26

Grid (numbers per cell; ■ = blocked cell):

	16	■	13	9	6	20	24	16	21	■	3	
19	6	10	10	■	16	■	11	■	2	17	10	1
■	22	■	20	16	11	3 (M)	20	16	13	■	6	■
7	9	16	4 (P)	■	8	■	21	■	20	14	9	24
■	11	■	■	20	15	10	5	■	11	■	10	
5	10	20	11	■	6	■		18	9	20	6	
16	■	3	20	25	20	12	16	6	10	1	■	10
24	23	20	17	■	■	■	6	■	1	23	9	24
21	■	12	■	16	21	10	5	■	■	6		
23	2	10	1	■	11	■	9	■	16	6	26	2
■	8	■	10	6	20 (A)	14	13	10	5	■	2	■
3	10	17	13	■	26	■	25	■	10	10	13	1
■	6	■	13	10	24	24	10	11	1	■	5	■

A B C D E F G H I J K L M
N O P Q R S T U V W X Y Z

1	2	3	4	5	6	7	8	9	10	11	12	13
		M	P									

14	15	16	17	18	19	20	21	22	23	24	25	26
						A						

Codeword 74

	12		26		21		22		22		19	
6	22	8	19	8	19		21	4	18	19	8	12
	26		20		8	17	21		22		2	
13	22	11	11	4	7		4		20	24	24	10
	20				19	9	23				11	
7	19	16	16	24		19		6 P	24	15	4	20
		4		26	22	3	3	12		22		
2	25	22	20	16		3		19	8	7	4	5
	22				7	22 A	21				1	
2	14	22	20		19		22	20	11	26	17	3
	22		17 U		22	19	7		22		19	
6	20	4	26	4	20		18	20	17	11	6	23
	7		26		23		4		3		12	

A B C D E F G H I J K L M
N O P Q R S T U V W X Y Z

1	2	3	4	5	6	7	8	9	10	11	12	13
14	15	16	17	18	19	20	21	22	23	24	25	26

Codeword 75

	18		11		20		18		6		11	
19	16	13	20	8	2		23	24	9	20	21	20
	26		8		24		1		23		23	
15	16	21	7		13	22	7	13	16	20	18	11
	8				20		20		7		16	
4	22	10	10 M	9	21	23	7	23	16	11		
	14		20						11		4	
	16	17	14 P	8	20	21	20	7	22	5	12	
	24		23		23 I		22				9	
16	8	16	10	16	21	7	11		2	5	16	16
	16		23		1		13		8		8	
18	20	3	3	8	16		16	25	16	4	7	11
	21		16		18		11		18		12	

A B C D E F G H I J K L M
N O P Q R S T U V W X Y Z

1	2	3	4	5	6	7	8	9	10	11	12	13
14	15	16	17	18	19	20	21	22	23	24	25	26

Codeword 76

		3		23		18		2		5		12 **S**
	15	11	26	1	18	15		20	14	3	22	5
		23		12		7	15	18		25		3
15	19	1	9	20	17 **T**			1	25	25	20	18
12			15				20		3		1	
21	1	4	11	1	4		13	20	11	1	11	
8		20			15	12	5			19		1
	20	24	20	26	8		1	11	16	15	18	23
	19		18		12				1			23 **D**
5	20	17	15	24		17	1	6	20	11	12	
20		15		3	5	12		1		26		
12	1	24	20	12		22	10	5	3	26	11	
17		6		21		18		12		8		

A	B	C	D	E	F	G	H	I	J	K	L	M
N	O	P	Q	R	S	T	U	V	W	X	Y	Z

1	2	3	4	5	6	7	8	9	10	11	12	13
14	15	16	17	18	19	20	21	22	23	24	25	26

Codeword 77

24		3		8		3		24		12		17
9	11	4	2	24		17	19	14	21	24	1	2
1		2		16		6		20		5		17 **E**
13	5	1	16	16	21	17		7 **U**	2	25	17	5
17		3				9		24				12
9	10	24	12	15	17	11	11	1		11	4	17
		11		24				3		5		
17	23	17		3	1	12	15	11	2	24	5	17
3				12		24				26		24
5	15	1	3	4		21	24	6	18	17	5	9
4		21		26		4		24		9		1
25	17	21	1	17	22	9 **S**		9	24	11	1	3
17		9		5		15		10		18		12

A	B	C	D	E	F	G	H	I	J	K	L	M
N	O	P	Q	R	S	T	U	V	W	X	Y	Z

1	2	3	4	5	6	7	8	9	10	11	12	13
14	15	16	17	18	19	20	21	22	23	24	25	26

Codeword 78

5	10	22	3	■	5	■	23 P	■	19	8	5	14
21 L	■	16	■	8	24	19	12	26	■	21	■	16
18 M	16	21	9	■	19	■	16	■	15	3	19	21
8	■	21	16	14	12	■	17	5	12	6	■	5
■	5	■	21	■	6	12	6	■	10	■	16	■
5	11	23	3	8	5	■	8	4	5	12	6	8
■	19	■	■	16	■	■	■	3	■	■	10	■
12	26	25	16	8	5	■	4	3	14	6	22	2
■	5	■	13	■	8	9	16	■	16	■	2	■
12	■	1	16	17	10	■	26	19	15	15	■	8
13	12	12	8	■	14	■	5	■	15	5	5	6
5	■	17	■	20	3	16	8	6	■	17	■	12
6	3	2	8	■	4	■	6	■	5	26	7	2

A	B	C	D	E	F	G	H	I	J	K	L	M
N	O	P	Q	R	S	T	U	V	W	X	Y	Z

1	2	3	4	5	6	7	8	9	10	11	12	13
14	15	16	17	18	19	20	21	22	23	24	25	26

5	1	3	15	24	■	7	13	19	2	19	6	20
■	3	■	1	■	7	■	19	■	10	■	1	■
26	3	7	16	19	8	7	24	■	26	10	2	24
■	10	■	16	■	26	■	5	■	1	■	11	■
2	9	7	25	23	7	■	3 **R**	1	21	10	3	■
■	■	7	■	5	■	19	■	■	■	1	■
26	1	2	24	■	2	10	4	■	18	11	25	14
■	5	■	■	1	■	19	■	19	■		
■	22	11	7	24	2	■	6	7	24	2	7	13
■	11	■	1	■	19	■	1	■	2	■	23	■
12	19	20 **G**	24	■	10	11	2	5	10	4	7	24
■	2	■	7	■	6	■	7	■	3	■	6 **N**	■
11	24	7	25	7	24	24	■	5	17	24	2	24

A	B	C	D	E	F	G	H	I	J	K	L	M
N	O	P	Q	R	S	T	U	V	W	X	Y	Z

1	2	3	4	5	6	7	8	9	10	11	12	13
14	15	16	17	18	19	20	21	22	23	24	25	26

16	18	2	13	3	14			23		8	21	10
	2		2		1		7	26	21	2		2
12	26	11	21	16	3	26		2		2	17	14
	19			2		3	10	2			19	
19	17 (L)	10	3	7	26	19		22	3	3	14	16
14		24		3		23			20		17	
16	15	11	19	26	3		4	3	19	20	3	14
	11		14			25		18		3		11
18	19	6	2	26		3	5	23	17	19 (A)	21 (I)	24
	12			3	19	20		20			24	
16	13	1		24		16	2	1	7	3	19	24
13		11	16	3	14		19		1		23	
19	21	18		9			20	9	3	24	20	1

A	B	C	D	E	F	G	H	I	J	K	L	M
N	O	P	Q	R	S	T	U	V	W	X	Y	Z

1	2	3	4	5	6	7	8	9	10	11	12	13
14	15	16	17	18	19	20	21	22	23	24	25	26

Codeword 81

24	■	16	■	16	■	20	■	23	■	18	■	23
2	13 **P**	20	3	8	10	19	■	20	16	12	23	2
11	■	15	■	10	■	12	■	22 **T**	■	17	■	2
10	22	26	2	18	■	20	14	10	17	23	10	9
19	■	12	■	6	■	■	■	20	■	■	■	7
■	12	17	9	12	14	12	9	8	20	6	6	25
18	■	10	■	■	19	■	■	■	20	■	10	
8	17	18	8 **U**	15	15	10	18	18	21	8	6	■
15	■	■	26	■	■	■	11	■	17	■	7	
15	2	17	22	10	1	22	■	12	17	15	8	19
10	■	20	■	4	■	2	■	17	■	26	■	20
18	10	12	5	10	■	4	20	17	9	10	19	18
18	■	6	■	9	■	18	■	25	■	9	■	18

A B C D E F G H I J K L M
N O P Q R S T U V W X Y Z

1	2	3	4	5	6	7	8	9	10	11	12	13
14	15	16	17	18	19	20	21	22	23	24	25	26

Codeword 82

1	■	17	■	15			■	20	■	10		26
14	10	25	6	12	2	2	■	8	18	8	17	25
14	■	1	■	17	■	6	■	20 **P**	■	7		14
25	6	6	■	25	24	13	12	20	7	25	17	19
7	■	■	■	1	■	14	■	25	■	16	■	■
9	12	19	25	6	■	19	25	11	12	8	13	14
15	■	6	■	■	■	6	■	■	■	6	■	12
25	23	8	19	12	21	1	■	22	8	4	25	11
■	■	13	■	17	■	19	■	8	■	■	■	25
1	7	9	12	3	13	12	19	5	■	9	8	16
12	■	15	■	25	■	8	■	2	■	1		1
11	25	25	7	14	■	17 **N**	1	13 **U**	3	10	19	5
14	■	14	■	19			■	15	■	19		14

A	B	C	D	E	F	G	H	I	J	K	L	M
N	O	P	Q	R	S	T	U	V	W	X	Y	Z

1	2	3	4	5	6	7	8	9	10	11	12	13

14	15	16	17	18	19	20	21	22	23	24	25	26

Codeword 83

	22		26		7		18		17		7
22	3	14	22	18	22		16	26	22	17	9
	17		15		4	22	10		20		1
18	3	16	21	9	7			22	10	13	21	21
16			14			12		13		16	
23	22	15	22	15	22		22	21	18	16	17
21		9		15	9	6			6		12
	7	9	17	7	16		24	13	19	15	9	11
	9		9		15				16		14
9	26	9	15	21			10	16	21	5	2	9
20		26		3	22	6		11		2	
22	19	13	9	2		16	14	9	7	22	21
		I		**U**							
10		3		25		6		8		19	
				G							

A	B	C	D	E	F	G	H	I	J	K	L	M
N	O	P	Q	R	S	T	U	V	W	X	Y	Z

1	2	3	4	5	6	7	8	9	10	11	12	13
14	15	16	17	18	10	20	21	22	23	24	25	26

Codeword 84

	25		3		3		8		14		14	
14	9	13	11	14	16		9	6	7	14	16	10
	7		18		11	23	25		13		5	
3	13	23	18	9	25		23 **O**		14	4	14	13
	14			19 **G**	12	2					16	
24	16	11	2	26		7		14	8	23	11	15
	16		13	14	24	5	10		3			
24	9	16	16	23		24		5	23	3	17	14
	1			10	14	24				14		
22	11	17	10		21		23	26	4	9	24	17
	10		5		9	2	7		23		5	
10	17	13	11	5	9		24	14	16	16	9	15
	10		22		17		20		17		15	

A	B	C	D	E	F	G	H	I	J	K	L	M
N	O	P	Q	R	S	T	U	V	W	X	Y	Z

1	2	3	4	5	6	7	8	9	10	11	12	13
14	15	16	17	18	19	20	21	22	23	24	25	26

Codeword 85

	19		7		8		9		10		13	
15	25	23	17	25 (E)	22		7	6	7	23	25	7
	4		20		22		11		24		2	
1	7	20	25		9	11	19	14	7	10	10	9
	3				25		25		14		12	
18	8	24	13	9	12	7	12	17	8	14		
	14		14					17		9 (S)	
	11	8	14	11	25	17	21	7	15	23	16
	26		11		19		24			5	
24	5	11	13	9	7	11	13		8 (O)	2	17	12
	7		17		17		17		7		11	
18	17	14	14	25	24		14	5	24	9	25	9
	23		3		9		3		9		9	

A	B	C	D	E	F	G	H	I	J	K	L	M
N	O	P	Q	R	S	T	U	V	W	X	Y	Z

1	2	3	4	5	6	7	8	9	10	11	12	13
14	15	16	17	18	19	20	21	22	23	24	25	26

Codeword 86

26	9	22	2	3	6		25	12	3	2	8	20 **G**
8		23		7				3		8		3
7	21	21		2	8	10	21	19	26	8	17	26
16		2		21		3		8				7
26	7	12	25		14	26	21	17	23	16 **M**	26	25
21		2		19		13		7		23		6
		17	23	8	4	19	17	12	23	3		
7		7		21		26		26		12		2
18	2	21	21	2	23	8	25		1	7	2	8
21				15		17		5		21		12
7	3	17	11	26	12	6	22	26		2	3	26
24		23		21				25		12		8
26	25	25	7	6	25		25	12	7	6	26	4 **D**

| A | B | C | D | E | F | G | H | I | J | K | L | M |
| N | O | P | Q | R | S | T | U | V | W | X | Y | Z |

1	2	3	4	5	6	7	8	9	10	11	12	13
14	15	16	17	18	19	20	21	22	23	24	25	26

Codeword 87

	21	24	18	7	17	14	3		10	7	23	7
7		21		11		24				8		24
11	10	19	23	10	18 **R**	12		4	8	9	10	20
9		4		23		14		15		4		24
6	10	18	5	4		19	9	5	20	4	14	
6				17		4		4		13		7
4	25	3	20	24	26		9	3	23	4	4	3
12		18		20 **L**		10		11				18
	16	24 **O**	14	12	4	12		14	25	1	9	4
9		2		4		12		24		24		10
7	21	4	10	18		14	22	19	24	18	4	12
4		5				19		10		4		7
7	14	11	4		10	22	4	20	4	7	7	

A	B	C	D	E	F	G	H	I	J	K	L	M
N	O	P	Q	R	S	T	U	V	W	X	Y	Z

1	2	3	4	5	6	7	8	9	10	11	12	13
14	15	16	17	18	19	20	21	22	23	24	25	26

Codeword 88

	21		21		16		17		3		6
	10	19	13	12	7	19		5	17	24	7	25
		20		16		11 U	22	15		6		20
13	19	9	10	19	22			19	26	26	5	23
24			24				18		12		13	
22 P	19	14 G	24	9	19		11	20	2	5	22
12		24			15	12	19			26		9
	26	24	7	16	8		25	12	19	15	16	25
	12		12		25				14			12
21	12	12	26	25			21	6	24	10	4	15
5		7		19	15	22		5		11		
16	8	7	24	3		12	1	12	10	16	15	
15		15		15		10		15		12		

A B C D E F G H I J K L M
N O P Q R S T U V W X Y Z

1	2	3	4	5	6	7	8	9	10	11	12	13
14	15	16	17	18	19	20	21	22	23	24	25	26

Codeword 89

24	4	7	15	11	5		18	20	11	8	23	11
1		11		23		18 A		11		1		20
8	11	24	1	23	11	23		14	1	8	23	11
3		18		18		19		5		18		8
	8	1	25	3		11 E	2	1	18	10	10	3
23		10				26		8				9
9	1	5	16	1	5		8	11	13	9	4	14
10 L				16		23				7		11
7	11	10	4	15	12	5		19	11	3	23	
4		18		8		9		14		23		11
11	22	5	8	18		21	8	9	23	23	11	7
8		11		7		19		26		11		15
23	11	8	4	11	23		11	14	6	3	17	11

A B C D E F G H I J K L M
N O P Q R S T U V W X Y Z

1	2	3	4	5	6	7	8	9	10	11	12	13
14	15	16	17	18	19	20	21	22	23	24	25	26

Codeword 90

	25		4		3		12		8		19	
26	1	16	21	5	1 **U**		16	21	12	17	21	23
	18		16		3	21	21		12		10	
2	11	16	21	14	3		5		19	8	1	13
	8				11	17	15				21	
14	16	5	20	21		5		5	7	13	17	21
		2		9	21	16	26	19		4		
19	3	8	18	21		9		4	5	11	16	24
	1				26	5	5				21	
5	18	3 **T**	21		17		22	16	8	18	6	19
	11		14		8	9	5		18		11	
5	18	24	4	8	22		19	5	17	5	7	11
	6 **G**		8		19		4		24		21	

A	B	C	D	E	F	G	H	I	J	K	L	M
N	O	P	Q	R	S	T	U	V	W	X	Y	Z

1	2	3	4	5	6	7	8	9	10	11	12	13
14	15	16	17	18	19	20	21	22	23	24	25	26

Codeword 91

4	17	5	12	■	20	■	18	■	9	2	16 **O**	12
9	■	12	■	13	17	13	24	3	■	9	■	9
26	4	9	23	■	3	■	12	■	9	5	5	13
12	■	10	16	17	2	■	9	21	4	15	■	12
■	20	■	4	■	5	16	26	■	12	■	6	■
14	9	17	25	26	13	■	13	7	9	18	12	13
■	23	■	■	12	■	■	■	9	■	■	19	■
1	17	16	26	9	13	■	3	25	10	16	4	23
■	26	■	3	■	24	12	25	■	9	■	9	■
10	■	23	12	13	9	■	22	16	21	13	■	12
12	4 **R**	9	13	■	8	■	12	■	25	9	22	15
26	■	6	■	19	12	9	25	13	■	20 **G**	■	12
9	11	12	5	■	25	■	26	■	7	9	3	5

A B C D E F G H I J K L M
N O P Q R S T U V W X Y Z

1	2	3	4	5	6	7	8	9	10	11	12	13
14	15	16	17	18	19	20	21	22	23	24	25	26

Codeword 92

	8	7	1	17	14	20	1		19	21	26	21
7		23		14		4			14		21	
3	14	20	21	18		20	25	16	10	17	4	1
21		7		5		14		4			2	
18	14	10	2		14	8	7	11	25	14	1	7
13		1		2		14		25 U		15		
	8	4	17	1	13		5	21	21	15	13	
		21		17		20		17		7		8
2	25	18	16 L	4	5	12	1		2	20	14	17
	18			10		21		2		1		4
14	8	9	4	2	7	2 S		10	17	4	6	7
	7		21			7		7		21		8
24	17	7	18		22	18	21	24	4	18	5	

A B C D E F G H I J K L M
N O P Q R S T U V W X Y Z

1	2	3	4	5	6	7	8	9	10	11	12	13
14	15	16	17	18	19	20	21	22	23	24	25	26

Codeword 93

6		9		19		25		10		15		25
15	13	8	10	11		16	22	23	15	11	22	11
13		26		18		14		16		16		20
25 R	26	17	13	22	22 T	16		19	8	24	12	11
11		3				12		12				17
22	21	11	19	22	26	11	22	23		17	8	22
		10		7				16		25		
1	11	22		2	8	4	15	26	17	26	5	11
16				11		11				22		25
7	11	16	25	10		23	11	16	14	26	11	25
23		25		11		11		1		17		16
11	18	17	26	22	11	10		2	25	16 A	21	19
1		23		10		22		10		15		24

A	B	C	D	E	F	G	H	I	J	K	L	M
N	O	P	Q	R	S	T	U	V	W	X	Y	Z

1	2	3	4	5	6	7	8	9	10	11	12	13
14	15	16	17	18	19	20	21	22	23	24	25	26

Codeword 94

18	14	5	6	19	■	11	18	19	5	9	16	14
■	18	■	17	■	14	■	5	■	6	■	8	■
20	26	3	23 **L**	6	26	1	9	■	3	6	26	19
■	7	■	22	■	3	■	22	■	1	■	18	■
9	18	7	1	16	3	■	16	25	22	5	19	■
■	■	■	16	■	6	■	15	■	■	■	6	■
10	22	12	14	■	26 **U**	14	16	■	19	26	3	20
■	7	■	■	■	7	■	11	■	4	■	■	■
■	2	6	21	16	25	■	16	24	12	22	3	16
■	26	■	7	■	22	■	7	■	22	■	16	■
18	3	22	18	■	7	6	19	22	5	22	7	1 **G**
■	16	■	15	■	1	■	14	■	18	■	16	■
18	25	15	16	3	14	16	■	5	23	6	13	7

A B C D E F G H I J K L M
N O P Q R S T U V W X Y Z

1	2	3	4	5	6	7	8	9	10	11	12	13
14	15	16	17	18	19	20	21	22	23	24	25	26

	21		19		6		7		22		23
2	9	19	9	3 **E**	12		26	12	13	22	3
	3		13		22	7	12		12		3
20	21	25	7	15	14		7	16	22	3	25
7			19			5		7		7	
20	12	21	3	25	18	3	15	22	3	25	
11		3		7	5	3			5		7
	18	7	22	4	11		17	13	24	3	15	20
	13		7		22			9			21
11	7	12	15	22		18	1	21	7	20	20
3		15		13	25	3		12		15	
7	8	9 **I**	13	2		15 **N**	9	4	10	3	17
19		22		18		17		10		5	

| A | B | C | D | E | F | G | H | I | J | K | L | M |
| N | O | P | Q | R | S | T | U | V | W | X | Y | Z |

1	2	3	4	5	6	7	8	9	10	11	12	13
14	15	16	17	18	19	20	21	22	23	24	25	26

Codeword 96

25	4	4	20		14		2		6	22	3	26 **E**
3		1		22	25	4	14	24		11		3
11	19	26	13		21		4		11	20	13	22
1		12	26	24	11		24	11	16	6		26
	8		18		24	6	26		3		11	
21	4 **O**	24	11	18	26		22	13	26	3	3	1
	3			26				4			6	
23	3	11	13	26	22		9	11	24	6	5	26
	1		4		25 **P**	19	6		15		26	
22		26	15	26	20		10	20	6	4		4
7	6	3	9		1		10		18	9	11	15
6		13		22	3	1	3	1		17		3
25	26	22	24		1		26		9	26	24	22

A	B	C	D	E	F	G	H	I	J	K	L	M
N	O	P	Q	R	S	T	U	V	W	X	Y	Z

1	2	3	4	5	6	7	8	9	10	11	12	13
14	15	16	17	18	19	20	21	22	23	24	25	26

Codeword 97

	16		23		8		14		12		9	
26	4	13	4	13	4		7	13	2	1	14	18
	1		19		1		10		8		14	
5	2	19	19		14	12	14	22 **P**	3	4	13	1
	10				4		21		1		15	
18	2	16	6	11	7	10	4	8	14	18		
	6		11						16		7	
	2	13	16	1	10	7	6	1	2	13	8	
	6		1		3		13				18	
24	7	4	10	1	14	10	16 **S**		9	11	11	5
	10 **R**		4		25		4		4		2	
4	17	14	10	16	14		5	2	20	2	13	8
	14		15		16		14		15		8	

A	B	C	D	E	F	G	H	I	J	K	L	M
N	O	P	Q	R	S	T	U	V	W	X	Y	Z

1	2	3	4	5	6	7	8	9	10	11	12	13
14	15	16	17	18	19	20	21	22	23	24	25	26

20	6	6	15	4	7	■	■	6	■	6	19	7
	24	■	24	■	13	■	17	12	7	26	■	11
14	15	20	4	6	15	13	■	6	■	19	9	9
■	16	■	■	2	■	12	11	11	■	■	24	
16	6	20	6	12	19	4	■	7	20	17	7	16
12	■	5 **D**	■	7	■	25	■	■	6	■	7	■
13	19	5	12	9	10	■	3	24	7	7	5	10
■	21	■	4	■	■	21	■	7	■	20	■	20
8	7	20	4	16	■	11	7	4	3	6	2	10
	10	■	■	1	24	19 **O**	■	20	■	■	7	■
1	16	12	■	24	■	22	19	11	11	15 **U**	5	7
7	■	13	7	7	18	■	17	■	7	■	3	
3	20	1	■	7	■	■	20	13	20	23	7	16

A	B	C	D	E	F	G	H	I	J	K	L	M
N	O	P	Q	R	S	T	U	V	W	X	Y	Z

1	2	3	4	5	6	7	8	9	10	11	12	13
14	15	16	17	18	19	20	21	22	23	24	25	26

Codeword 99

	3		9		6		24		24	
25	12	11	7	2		19	2	2	20	2	10
9		18		6		11		4		11		11
16	2	12	19	16	2	10		2	17	23	25	19
2		8		6		2		26				1
18	2	2	8		16		10	2	16	11	25	8 **L**
22		6		18	1	13	11	8		16		1
2	11	6	25	2	18		9		6	16	11	7
9				21		23		1		18		25
2	14	25	8	2		19	25	15	15	11	15	15
6		8		18 **R**		6 **S**		1		5		2
	11	8	8	2	7	2		9	1	16	2	10
		6		2		16		2		6		

A	B	C	D	E	F	G	H	I	J	K	L	M
N	O	P	Q	R	S	T	U	V	W	X	Y	Z

1	2	3	4	5	6	7	8	9	10	11	12	13
14	15	16	17	18	19	20	21	22	23	24	25	26

Codeword 100

	3	17	14	3	17	23	26		21	26	12	6
26		20 M		8		26			17		17	
1	8	17	24	14		3	15	8	12	4	10	8
1		10		24		17		12			8	
26	9	4	3			17	23	13	4	14	26	12	14 S
23		2		11		26		16		7		
	17	16	19	8	25		2	4	26	3	26	
		19		18		25		2		19		14
23	17	5	23	12	26	17	20		22	18	4	24
	13			24		23		25		14		17
12	26	17	3	15	26	23		4	3	4	2	16
	12		17			19		6		13		5
14	24 T	18	23		23	26	12	4	13	26	14	

A	B	C	D	E	F	G	H	I	J	K	L	M
N	O	P	Q	R	S	T	U	V	W	X	Y	Z

1	2	3	4	5	6	7	8	9	10	11	12	13
14	15	16	17	18	19	20	21	22	23	24	25	26

Codeword 101

	9		24		2		25		26		11
	1	20	5	20	1	13		14	18	6	13	4
		17		1		23	13	9		4		14
9	14	3 **S**	24	14	16			8	26	4	14	16
14			13				7		8		7	
13	5	5	6	13	4		13	16	8	9	14	
17		20			19	6 **U**	1			6		6
	11	4	8	23	5		17	4	13	5	14	3
	4		13		12				1 **M**			14
10	6	21	22	3			17	14	17	17	14	9
13		4		8	5	14		13		6		
21	15	13	11	11		1	14	24	14	9	3	
22		19		13		8		3		14		

A	B	C	D	E	F	G	H	I	J	K	L	M
N	O	P	Q	R	S	T	U	V	W	X	Y	Z

1	2	3	4	5	6	7	8	9	10	11	12	13
14	15	16	17	18	19	20	21	22	23	24	25	26

Codeword 102

7	20	19	14	7	21		7	6	19	12	12	7
	19		7		14		5		17		9	
15	9	16	15 **P**	15	9	7	7	5	22	24	4	
	6		21	15			6		8			
7	14	24	14	16	5	18	5	11	2	11	1 **R**	
		24		17	11			1				
3	11	7	6	11	25	25		8	19	7	26	
	13			7	11		1					
14	23	1	9	7 **S**	7	6	1	5	18	5	14	
	24		18		14		10		17			
23	14	6	14	23	9	16	22	10	11	14	24	
	5		6	24		24		24		17		
5	16	15	11	17	8	11	18	11	17	11	8	

A	B	C	D	E	F	G	H	I	J	K	L	M
N	O	P	Q	R	S	T	U	V	W	X	Y	Z

1	2	3	4	5	6	7	8	9	10	11	12	13
14	15	16	17	18	19	20	21	22	23	24	25	26

Codeword 103

	5		8		15		9		13 (T)		14	
11	2	1	6	21	12		17	6	14	5	17	12
	26		3		5	12	12		3		7	
19	12	3	4	10	26		12		9	17	14	5
	14				14	9	11				17	
24	2	21	21	14		7		10	26	5	6	13
		18		26	10	2	25	18		10		
22	2	6	21	7		17		1	6	16	12	9
	3				12	17	8				23	
2	17	3	14		1		17	14	26	25	12	26
	12		1		12	20	12		12		21	
6	9	10 (S)	1 (O)	12	26		12	16	14	17	13	9
	9		10		24		13		26		9	

A	B	C	D	E	F	G	H	I	J	K	L	M
N	O	P	Q	R	S	T	U	V	W	X	Y	Z

1	2	3	4	5	6	7	8	9	10	11	12	13
14	15	16	17	18	19	20	21	22	23	24	25	26

Codeword 104

16	21 U	15	15		18		22		26	16	26	18
21		3		22	19	25	19	9		20		26
7	3	3	25		23		26		25	10	20	4
5		2	19	11	21		12	3	20	4		19
	3		19		19	3	11		4		26	
13	20	7	5	20	9		18	25	10	19	22	19
	18			10				18			5	
5	26	24	11	20	25		16	26	20	18	19	24
	18		19		19	2	21		9		24	
9		11	3	1	20		24	3	9	4 T		24
3	14	19 E	11		11		12		6	3	5	19
20		8		7	21	22	19	18		17		17
11	3	18	6		4		4		26	17	17	6

A B C D E F G H I J K L M
N O P Q R S T U V W X Y Z

1	2	3	4	5	6	7	8	9	10	11	12	13

14	15	16	17	18	19	20	21	22	23	24	25	26

Codeword 105

■	23	26	17	24	20	17	22	■	22	24	15	26
24	■	24	■	4	■	24	■	18	■	12	■	8
19	17	23	16	2	17	15	■	14	12	9	8	1
16	■	13	■	8	■	8	■	24	■	17	■	9
22 **R**	8	15	17	12	■	1	8	12	8	12	5	■
9	■	■	■	8	■	7	■	9	■	12	■	24 **A**
17	6	20	16	15	17	■	11	8	25	24	22	4
4	■	22	■	9 **T**	■	26	■	21	■	■	■	10
■	1	16	10	17	1	7	■	8	12	4	8	17
9	■	21	■	22	■	15	■	24	■	16	■	22
11	26	8	1	17	■	15	14	19	3	17	23	9
8	■	9	■	4	■	16	■	1	■	22	■	15
5	14	15	26	■	24	20	20	17	24	15	17	■

A	B	C	D	E	F	G	H	I	J	K	L	M
N	O	P	Q	R	S	T	U	V	W	X	Y	Z

1	2	3	4	5	6	7	8	9	10	11	12	13
14	15	16	17	18	19	20	21	22	23	24	25	26

4		25		4		1		14		1		18
18	9	15	14	25	18	16		16	11	25 **I**	18	6
17		18		14		16		13		22		16
26	5	25	15	7		4	14	10	23	25	19	16
5		8		6				25				14
	25	15	6	16	14	3	25	15 **N**	7	24	19	16
18		25				10				25		21
5	16	7	21	2	9	7	14	6	16	14	18	
10				9				9		6		7
22	16	19	26	10	3	16		14	16	5	7	24
24		7		6		15		6		21		24
25	3 **M**	24	9	16		12	10	19	26	7	15	10
20		18		21		17		16		17		6

A B C D E F G H I J K L M
N O P Q R S T U V W X Y Z

1	2	3	4	5	6	7	8	9	10	11	12	13
14	15	16	17	18	19	20	21	22	23	24	25	26

	1	19	19	25	12	17	20		5	18	1	13
6		14		16		18			26		26	
18	11	1	15 **M**	20		19	10	21	10	2	18	4
14		12		21		18		1			1	
14	25	10	4		16	4	20	21	18	1	17	9
9		3		21		21		21		17		
	20	10	22	26	21		8	25	25	17	20	
	18		10		3		25		10			20
16	4	17	18	12 **R**	14	10	18		1	19	26	18
	18 **E**			20		17		1		21		19
1	8	1	10	21	18	17		7	16	10	18	21
	18		14			14		16		23		20
21	12	18	13		17	18	24	1	21	18	17	

A	B	C	D	E	F	G	H	I	J	K	L	M
N	O	P	Q	R	S	T	U	V	W	X	Y	Z

1	2	3	4	5	6	7	8	9	10	11	12	13
14	15	16	17	18	19	20	21	22	23	24	25	26

Codeword 108

8	24	15	20	2	13	■	5	24	15	1	21	8
■	19	■	24	■	6	■	11	■	1	■	17	■
4	24	12	25	■	12	21	5	19	11	20	21	18
■	21	■	3	■	19	■	■	23	■	14	■	
3	18	11	6	26	1	■	10 P	18	21	9	2	14
■	■	■	18	■	3	■	21	■	■	■	13	■
20	21	16	21	■	24	11	12	■	15	11	13	21
■	7	■	■	■	20	■	2	■	19	■	■	
12	6	2	12	19	21	■	13	11	11	22	21	8
■	2	■	2	■	■	■	3	■	18	■	25	■
26 G	13	2	8	24	11	13	24	■	24	11	3	2
■	13	■	24	■	8	■	21 E	■	12	■	18	■
1	17	14	18	24	8	■	15	24	26	12	2	13

A	B	C	D	E	F	G	H	I	J	K	L	M
N	O	P	Q	R	S	T	U	V	W	X	Y	Z

1	2	3	4	5	6	7	8	9	10	11	12	13
14	15	16	17	18	19	20	21	22	23	24	25	26

Codeword 109

	24	17	6	3	18	11	23		9	2	6	24
17		10		9		16				17		6
25	10	11	13	9	10	15		19	9	9	24	13
17		26		21		22		11		13		5
21	23	17	24	4		9	14	8	17	7	9	
9				8		3		24		24		1 **P**
2	17	6	3	10	15		13	3	11	11	20	9
15		10		3		2 **M**		17				24
	4	10	9	9	25	9		10	11 **O**	17	3	13
9		3		13		3		6		24		6
12	9	9	24	13		21	9	13	6	22	3	13
9		13				9		7		8		7
3	11	13	9		11	21	15	13	13	9	15	

A	B	C	D	E	F	G	H	I	J	K	L	M
N	O	P	Q	R	S	T	U	V	W	X	Y	Z

1	2	3	4	5	6	7	8	9	10	11	12	13
14	15	16	17	18	19	20	21	22	23	24	25	26

		26 O		15		1		5		24		11
	9	24	7	22	11	7		7	16	13	2	13
		7		13		24	18	12		17		23
7	2	16	7	6	18			7	17	17	13	21
1			20				15		18		11	
9	18	1	3	23	26		22	23 N	6	13	10	
20		26			2	26	7			23		22
	5	23	7	12	18		8	13	23	23	18	24
	26		1		19				22			14
17	13	16	18	8			25	22	23	14	16	18
13		19		26	17	17		14		16		
9	3	24 R	26	4		7	20	16	18	18	10	
20		18		23		21		19		18		

A	B	C	D	E	F	G	H	I	J	K	L	M
N	O	P	Q	R	S	T	U	V	W	X	Y	Z

1	2	3	4	5	6	7	8	9	10	11	12	13
14	15	16	17	18	19	20	21	22	23	24	25	26

Codeword 111

	12		6		12		17		10		16	
11	23	19	24	20	8		9	26	23	23	5	15
	5		5		4		21		11		22	
6	15	8	3		8	20	17	26	22	8	13 **T**	6
	5				20		26		8		26	
18	19	26	6	13	8	5	20	8	20	3		
	13		17						26		4	
	14	5	10	19	24	26	20	13	8	20	3	
	26		19		20		23				5	
26	2	21	23	5	14	26	14		25	11 **A**	10	4
	10		14		19		26		5		4	
22 **R**	26	7	26	11	23		6	26	8	1	26	14
	23		22		9		13		20		14	

A	B	C	D	E	F	G	H	I	J	K	L	M
N	O	P	Q	R	S	T	U	V	W	X	Y	Z

1	2	3	4	5	6	7	8	9	10	11	12	13
14	15	16	17	18	19	20	21	22	23	24	25	26

Codeword 112

	15	8	4	1	18	20	5		22	2	16	4
20		14		14		4		14		17		14
5	2	13	18	9 **G**	8	5		23	19	14	24	20
14		26 **D**		13		5		23		21		3
20	5	3	19	18		4	3	4	23	11	19 **L**	
8				23		4		15		4		25
4	12	2	5	18	15		20	5	4	6	4	2
26		6		15		20		18				19
	26	18	25	4	6	5		2	15	5	4	5
18		4		13		11		13		24		14
15	3	13	18	15		10	19	14	7	18	13	9
4		5		4		10		5		15		4
20	14	20	20		5	3	17	4	20	4	5	

A B C D E F G H I J K L M
N O P Q R S T U V W X Y Z

1	2	3	4	5	6	7	8	9	10	11	12	13
14	15	16	17	18	19	20	21	22	23	24	25	26

12	6	20	26	■	24	■	5	■	14	9	10	15
4	■	6	■	6	12	13	1	6	■	4	■	24
8	10	8	10	■	7	■	4	■	23	4	22	18
6	■	13	24	2	6	■	25	6	10	18	■	6 **E**
■	10	■	26	■	13	1	6	■	26	■	14	■
10	22	22	6	8	25	■	13	21	6	10	20	13
■	15	■	■	24	■	■	■	10	■	■	10	■
3	6	9	10	25 **T**	4	■	26	20	10	24	12	13
■	26	■	17	■	25	10	1	■	25	■	26	■
10	■	20	24	22	15	■	25	20	4	19	■	13
14	24	4	13	■	6	■	24	■	16 **M**	10	13	25
9	■	4	■	14	20	24	6	11	■	21	■	10
19	10	18	13	■	13	■	13	■	1	13	6	20

A	B	C	D	E	F	G	H	I	J	K	L	M
N	O	P	Q	R	S	T	U	V	W	X	Y	Z

1	2	3	4	5	6	7	8	9	10	11	12	13
14	15	16	17	18	19	20	21	22	23	24	25	26

Codeword 114

14	■	11	■	17	■	25	■	6	■	21	■	11
18	8	23	9	9	16	9	■	23	18	25	9	13
7	■	13	■	4	■	13	■	13	■	12		9
4	9	19	21	14	■	9	24	9	2	23	21	9
9 **E**	■	12	■	19	■		■	14	■	■	■	7
■	18	23	6	18	21	7	21	23	21	7	12	26
15 **P**	■	3 **G**	■	■	■	19	■	■	■	26	■	3
13	9	25	14	6	7	19	7	21	14	21	9	■
12	■	■	■	9	■	■	■	9	■	9	■	6
6	9	20	9	22	9	19	■	26	23	13	18	9
19	■	9	■	14	■	14	■	26	■	10	■	13
9	13	13	12	13	■	15	13	7	10	14	2	1
17	■	5	■	9	■	18	■	18	■	19		19

A B C D E F G H I J K L M
N O P Q R S T U V W X Y Z

1	2	3	4	5	6	7	8	9	10	11	12	13
14	15	16	17	18	19	20	21	22	23	24	25	26

Codeword 115

Grid letters given: 20 = G, 2 = U, 12 = P

A	B	C	D	E	F	G	H	I	J	K	L	M
N	O	P	Q	R	S	T	U	V	W	X	Y	Z

1	2	3	4	5	6	7	8	9	10	11	12	13
14	15	16	17	18	19	20	21	22	23	24	25	26

Codeword 116

	10		19		19		20		16		16	
14	16	15	5	4	3		14	1	12	6	19	2
	2		16		5	14	24		16		5	
1	6	21	14	16	24		6		7	14	8 **D**	6
	16				16	1	4				5	
26	17	14	2	16		16		11	5	2 **T**	19	3
		7		21	16	9	14	7		14		
19	3	6	16	22 **P**		14		9	17	21	21	9
	14			15	17	10				16		
22	25	6	16	14		5	24	13	5	2	6	
	25		24	7	6	13		6		7		
7	14	19	23	6	2		6	24	2	16	5	25
	11		3		9		24		14		18	

A B C D E F G H I J K L M
N O P Q R S T U V W X Y Z

1	2	3	4	5	6	7	8	9	10	11	12	13

14	15	16	17	18	19	20	21	22	23	24	25	26

A B C D E F G H I J K L M
N O P Q R S T U V W X Y Z

1	2	3	4	5	6	7	8	9	10	11	12	13
14	15	16	17	18	19	20	21	22	23	24	25	26

Codeword 118

		20		10		5		18		24		21
	18	9	23	18	3	24		4	25	23	13	22
		20		18		21	3	17		18		25
21	2	9	24	23	18			13	25	24	21	20
24			10				1		11		18	
8	25	10	10	25	16		17	15	24	5	18	
18		18			24	4	4			18		9
	22	24	4	4	19		21	22	17	6	18	21
	9		17		21				13			18
24	7	10	18	23 R			18	26	18	13	20	21
14		18		25	6	18		18		25		
10	25	5 G	17	13		24	20	20	18	6 N	12	
18		21		3		20		21		21		

A B C D E F G H I J K L M
N O P Q R S T U V W X Y Z

1	2	3	4	5	6	7	8	9	10	11	12	13

14	15	16	17	18	19	20	21	22	23	24	25	26

■	18	19	8	8	11	12	4	■	23	22	17	22
8	■	3	■	19	■	14	■	■	22	■	22	■
7	13	20	11	4	■	7	21	19	7	12	26	13
2	■	11	■	20	■	26	■	3	■	■	3	■
4	2	7	23	■	26	3	12	11	14	11	4	12
11	■	8	■	10	■	4	■	16	■	25	■	■
■	4	12	14	7	6	■	12	11	23	2	22	■
■	■	20	■	12	■	19	■	3	■	8	■	5 **D**
7	3	6	9	20	11	14	11	■	22	22	1	11
■	22	■	■	11	■	15	■	13	■	4	■	2
22	18	4	11	14	16	11 **E**	■	7	23	26	15	22
■	8	■	8	■	■	3 **N**	■	4	■	22	■	12
4	11	7	23	■	4	12	7	24	26	3	15	■

A	B	C	D	E	F	G	H	I	J	K	L	M
N	O	P	Q	R	S	T	U	V	W	X	Y	Z

1	2	3	4	5	6	7	8	9	10	11	12	13
14	15	16	17	18	19	20	21	22	23	24	25	26

Codeword 120

	11		3		10		9		6		5	
9	16	25	8	9	16		20	16	11	1	24	4
	10		4		1		12		16		8	
12	10	10	9		6	8	24	1	23	22	9	20
	22				12		24		23		12	
9	2	12	26	16	11	1	9	20	22	7		
	9		12						2		11	
		20	12	15	16	1	12	5	22 **I**	25	16	24
	11		14		17		24				7	
6	12	18	12	11	16	2	12		12	1	22	2
	5		18		24		21		25		1	
25 **M**	13 **U**	1	1	24	12		12	19	13	16	24	9
	11		9		16		18		9		4	

A	B	C	D	E	F	G	H	I	J	K	L	M
N	O	P	Q	R	S	T	U	V	W	X	Y	Z

1	2	3	4	5	6	7	8	9	10	11	12	13
14	15	16	17	18	19	20	21	22	23	24	25	26

Codeword 121

26	21	26	6	■	26	■	12	■	17	8	21	2
4	■	25	■	2	21	16	25	15 (L)	■	10	■	17
18	4	19	18	■	4	■	8	■	3	21	15	22
21	■	25	11	6	19	■	10	21	4	2	■	21
■	20	■	6	■	25	11	21	■	19	■	13	■
1	17	19	18	15	21	■	8	13	4 (A)	15	21	8
■	21	■	21	■	■	■	17	■	■	2	■
5	11	25	16	25	4	■	4	23	25	2	21	8
■	14	■	25	■	12	4	9	■	12	■	2	■
25	■	2	21	4	12	■	25	19	12	6	■	8
2	11 (R)	4	7	■	4	■	6	■	14	17	13	3
21	■	24	■	12	25	15	26	8	■	13	■	25
4	22	21	2	■	11	■	8	■	7	10	25	22

A	B	C	D	E	F	G	H	I	J	K	L	M
N	O	P	Q	R	S	T	U	V	W	X	Y	Z

1	2	3	4	5	6	7	8	9	10	11	12	13

14	15	16	17	18	19	20	21	22	23	24	25	26

Codeword 122

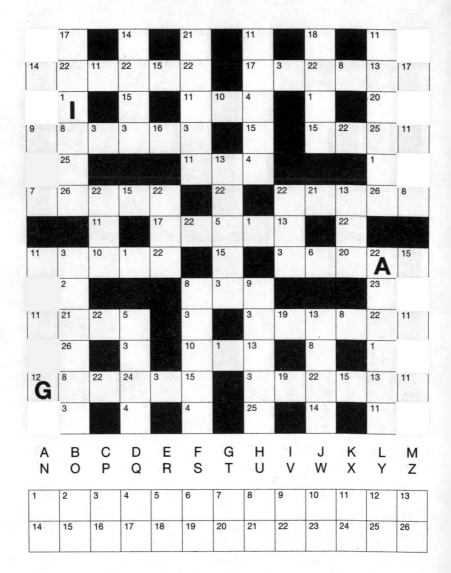

17		14		21		11		18		11	
14	22	11	22	15	22		17	3	22	8	13	17
	1 **I**		15		11	10	4		1		20	
9	8	3	3	16	3		15		15	22	25	11
	25				11	13	4				1	
7	26	22	15	22		22		22	21	13	26	8
		11		17	22	5	1	13		22		
11	3	10	1	22		15		3	6	20	22 **A**	15
	2				8	3	9				23	
11	21	22	5		3		3	19	13	8	22	11
	26		3		10	1	13		8		1	
12 **G**	8	22	24	3	15		3	19	22	15	13	11
	3		4		4		25		14		11	

A B C D E F G H I J K L M
N O P Q R S T U V W X Y Z

1	2	3	4	5	6	7	8	9	10	11	12	13
14	15	16	17	18	19	20	21	22	23	24	25	26

Codeword 123

	7	6	13			1	26	6		21		
	2		9	8	2	7		3	21	26	6	
18	9	19	20			15	26	12		23		
	25		18	9	13	13		3	6	23	26	
2	7	13	16		10			12		9	6	26
3			26	25	20		26	4	9		4	
6	9	9	2		3	9 O	12		1	20	15	13
	6		12	20	1		13	3	13			20
7	6	6		12			20		26	17	7	25
	13	9	12	13		5	26	26	2		25	
		11		7	6	9			14	3 I	7	23 L
	23	26	7	19		22	3	24	26		13	
		12		26	26	23				6	9	13

A	B	C	D	E	F	G	H	I	J	K	L	M
N	O	P	Q	R	S	T	U	V	W	X	Y	Z

1	2	3	4	5	6	7	8	9	10	11	12	13
14	15	16	17	18	19	20	21	22	23	24	25	26

Codeword 124

	18		15		19		5		11		8
24 **D**	5	1	6	9	5		17	23	9	18	3
	20		19		13	6	23		6		22
20	10	19	26	24	11		5	16	19	10	18
5		5				26		9		5	
13	5	16	10	9	20		9	10	19	8	12
3		5		4	5	7			9		21
	15	5	11	18	5		11	14	3	6	18	3 **E**
	11		25		10			3			11
10	9	7	9	24		24	9	25	18	5	18
9		23		5	6	15		20		10	
20	19	12	15	23		5	18	19	2	9	20
1		11		16		24		8 **N**		15	

A B C D E F G H I J K L M
N O P Q R S T U V W X Y Z

| 1 | 2 | 3 | 4 | 5 | 6 | 7 | 8 | 9 | 10 | 11 | 12 | 13 |
| 14 | 15 | 16 | 17 | 18 | 19 | 20 | 21 | 22 | 23 | 24 | 25 | 26 |

	25		4		11		1		10		22	
25	6	10	17	15	8		17	6 **N**	20	22	15	19
	15		22 **A**		22		25		26		24	
15	7	17	11		10	20	6	11	20	10	20	11
	22				23		20		22		3	
17	6	15	12	20	22	24	22	5	13	20		
	7		10						20		22	
		9	16	10	20	15	8	22	11	16	3	15
	12		23 **M**		18		25				20	
21	16	23	12	20	7	20	11		2	17	15	7
	13		7			20		11		22		16	
9	22	13	13	20	6		20	6	14	19	23	20
	10		19		11		6		14		20	

A B C D E F G H I J K L M
N O P Q R S T U V W X Y Z

1	2	3	4	5	6	7	8	9	10	11	12	13
14	15	16	17	18	19	20	21	22	23	24	25	26

Codeword 126

2	25	14	14		16		10		9	19	22	9
25 **A**		23		24	19	6	21	19		13		25
20	19	25	11		4		6		3	21	6	13
22		5	23	10	21		19	15	21	9		21
	17		18		19	14	15		17		18	
6	25	16	16	23	1		25	15 **M**	19	6	26	22
	9			16				23			26	
22	11	25	16	19	22		14	23	18 **U**	26	19	16
	22		19		7	23	21		6		16	
22		1	25	26	21		12	18	21	8		7
2	19	25	16		14		18		9	23	9	19
23		16		10	14	25	21	15		6		24
9	21	26	20		22		26		1	19	17	22

A B C D E F G H I J K L M
N O P Q R S T U V W X Y Z

1	2	3	4	5	6	7	8	9	10	11	12	13
14	15	16	17	18	19	20	21	22	23	24	25	26

25		7		5		19		6		19		12
15	26	17	19	12	24	26		22	3	2	11	3
26		12		17		26		3		1		23
26	4	5	26	17		25	24	2	1	1	17	26
7		21		22				11				24
	5	11	3	13	2	25	26	24	12	7	17	26
2		22				22				24		25
20 M	2	8	11	5	14	11	3	25	24	2	12	
9				14				24		23		9
24	26	18	26	12	17	13		11	8	14	26	24
26		12		3		17		23		8		12
13 S	9	24	2	23		26	10	22 U	12	17	17	16
13		16		26		25		26		16		13

A	B	C	D	E	F	G	H	I	J	K	L	M
N	O	P	Q	R	S	T	U	V	W	X	Y	Z

1	2	3	4	5	6	7	8	9	10	11	12	13
14	15	16	17	18	19	20	21	22	23	24	25	26

Codeword 128

	18		18		21		5		13		
9	6	17	1	14		14	6	11	11	1	14
20		17		14		18		26		10	1
14	1	14	1	18	15	9		25 **I**	10	15	1	4
18		5		3		17		5			20
19	1	18	10		17		13	6	20	6	14	1
11		24		2	5	7	1	9		10		14
1	24	8	5	1	15		12		6	15	5	10
14				18		9		22		1		18
14	25	26	18	23 **L**		16	6	18	14	14	1	23
3		1		5		6		14		23		23
	20	14	18	6	22	18		9	24	18	23	3
	11		9 **S**		15		8		3		

A	B	C	D	E	F	G	H	I	J	K	L	M
N	O	P	Q	R	S	T	U	V	W	X	Y	Z

1	2	3	4	5	6	7	8	9	10	11	12	13
14	15	16	17	18	19	20	21	22	23	24	25	26

18	5	11	24	20	16			7		12	20	5
	4		17		4		15	4	26	20		20
20	6	1	20	21	5	18		11		18	8	11
	23			17		3	11	18			25	
18	21	3	20	24	10	4		5	24	23	11	2
11		17		18		20			20		26	
16	20	19 **G**	24	20	20		5	4	13	13	20	20
	22		17			14		15		2		25
9	17	25	5	11		11	25	25	4	12	20	16
	23			2	17	19		20			25	
18	1	11		4		23	25	16	17	21	20	16
17		18 **S**	4	25	19		20		1		14	
20	2 **L**	8		20			20	18	18	11	12	18

A	B	C	D	E	F	G	H	I	J	K	L	M
N	O	P	Q	R	S	T	U	V	W	X	Y	Z

1	2	3	4	5	6	7	8	9	10	11	12	13
14	15	16	17	18	19	20	21	22	23	24	25	26

Codeword 130

7	8	1	20	24	4		11	1	24	20	16	14
	20		1		16		2		21		6	
26	16	23	11		22	3	1	5	20	16	6	25
	3		16		22		22		2		24	
4	16	23	14	2	24	20	24		24	8	2	1
	20				2		23		15			
9	12	25	1	20	24		23	19	24	3	13	24
			11		6		16				24	
5	14	19	24		20	2	1	15	18	1	6	24
	2		2		16		6		8		20	
15	5	19	5	2	5	17	5		2	1	8	20
	26		20		20		3		10		2	
22	3	24	24	14	24		23	14	5	3	24	4

(given letters in grid: R = 1, U = 8, D = 4)

A	B	C	D	E	F	G	H	I	J	K	L	M
N	O	P	Q	R	S	T	U	V	W	X	Y	Z

1	2	3	4	5	6	7	8	9	10	11	12	13
14	15	16	17	18	19	20	21	22	23	24	25	26

7		14		1		26		14		2		14
12	16	25	6	6		1	19	22	20	6	14	13
16		17		26		25		20		26		25
26	7	15	26	22	14	3		6	25	9	14	7
7		21				25		19				21
15	25	14	4	26	4	1	15	18		7	25	7
		14		11				14		8		
17	14	23		7	16	2	2	14	4	25	23	17
19				19		4				21		19
10	25	20	14	4		19	11	5	14	1	21 **T**	7
14		16		11		24		14		15		20 **P**
4	14	6	25	14	10	14		21	15	14	4	14
23		6		3		23 **N**		7		3		6

A	B	C	D	E	F	G	H	I	J	K	L	M
N	O	P	Q	R	S	T	U	V	W	X	Y	Z

1	2	3	4	5	6	7	8	9	10	11	12	13
14	15	16	17	18	19	20	21	22	23	24	25	26

Codeword 132

4		11		12		13		7		2		13
11	3	3	24	16	20	22 **G**		2	20	20	13	1
2		16		2		22		22		10		26
9	16	12	10	4		4	17	15	13	13	21	13
13		12		11				2				20
	25	13	8	3	20	4	10	19	2	10	13	4
2		15				2				18		13
5	15	19	13 **E**	2	15	11	19	2	10	16	11	
4				9				19 **R**		9		5
3	23	13	19	8	2	20		10	19	16	5	13
19		22		3		3		12		22		19
5	3	3	10	4		25	3	15	22	6	10	14
4		4		10		4		9		10		9

A	B	C	D	E	F	G	H	I	J	K	L	M
N	O	P	Q	R	S	T	U	V	W	X	Y	Z

1	2	3	4	5	6	7	8	9	10	11	12	13
14	15	16	17	18	19	20	21	22	23	24	25	26

Codeword 133

	18	7	3	11 **T**	3	14	22		26	21	14	24
12		3		20		9			18		1	
6	3	26	21	18		18	17	10	6	11	14	20
22 **N**		6		5		20		22			22	
2	6	12	26		15	6	9	11	10	20	18	7
14		21		24		26		10		18		
	9	3	8	3	18		6	15	10	11	18	
		22		22		6		5		20		13
14	20	16	6	22	3	1	18		21	3	20	6
	18			18		6		14		18		20
21	3	12	18	20	6	21		23	14	19	18	7
	16		23			18		3 **I**		6		25
3	22	4	14		18	6	20	11	13	21	25	

A B C D E F G H I J K L M
N O P Q R S T U V W X Y Z

1	2	3	4	5	6	7	8	9	10	11	12	13
14	15	16	17	18	19	20	21	22	23	24	25	26

Codeword 134

	8		7		24		20		19		14
6	13	18	20	8	2		5	23	13	21	26
	6		16		11	5	8		13		19
7	24	24	7	5	21		14	2	21	13	20 **N**
6			3			3		6		5	
7	15	25	2	22	16		13	24	24	7	6
10		7			5	21	4			12 **D**	10
	15	21	5	12	2		2	17	9	13	21	16
	13		20		10				6			2
14	7	22	4	10			7	20	26	14	13	3
26		13		16	7	20		7 **A**		7	
9	7	10	14	7		18	20	5	1	18	2
2		14		15		20		6		6	

A	B	C	D	E	F	G	H	I	J	K	L	M
N	O	P	Q	R	S	T	U	V	W	X	Y	Z

1	2	3	4	5	6	7	8	9	10	11	12	13
14	15	16	17	18	19	20	21	22	23	24	25	26

Codeword 135

12	19	23	8	26	13	■	8	6	23	13	7	8
	18	■	19	■	21	■	19	■	25	■	16	■
12	14	23	22	■	15	13	10	5	23	14	20	24
■	20	■	26	■	19	■	■	■	24	■	9	■
20	20	2	19	16	18	■	8	26	1	21	19	23
■	■	■	23	■	3	■	20	■	■	■	16	■
4	20	1	8	■	19	14	14	■	9	13	18	8
■	6	■	■	■	26	■	19	■	13	■	■	■
8	26	3	21	6	1	■	10	3	24	8	20	24
■	19	■	20	■	■	■	19	■	6 **P**	■	3	■
13	10	11	3	13	19	16	26	■	19	20	26	13
■	13	■	8	■	16	■	20	■	16	■	17 **D**	■
8	14	23	23	6	8	■	24 **R**	23	18	19	20	16

A	B	C	D	E	F	G	H	I	J	K	L	M
N	O	P	Q	R	S	T	U	V	W	X	Y	Z

1	2	3	4	5	6	7	8	9	10	11	12	13
14	15	16	17	18	10	20	21	22	23	24	25	26

Codeword 136

	11	■	21	■	11	■	8	■	18	■	6	■
14	3	12	2	17	5	■	23	21	11	18	14	25
	26	■	3	■	18	26	3	■	10	■	21	■
26	24	4	8	18	12	■	3	■	8	21	25	8
■	4	■	■	■	24	1	17	■	■	■	3	■
8	6	24	24	1	■	4	■	3	15	21	19	3
■	■	11	■	21	12	12	24	25	■	11	■	■
22	4	3	8	17	■	2	■	3	7	26	3	14
	12	■	■	■	16	18	6	■	■	■	20	■
8	26	4	19	■	3	■	21	12	17	5	3	13
	14 L	■	4	■	9	4	2	■	4	■	26	■
13	21	17 T	17	3	11	■	3	18	2	5	17	5
	19	■	25	■	21	■	19	■	8 S	■	8	■

A B C D E F G H I J K L M
N O P Q R S T U V W X Y Z

1	2	3	4	5	6	7	8	9	10	11	12	13
14	**15**	**16**	**17**	**18**	**19**	**20**	**21**	**22**	**23**	**24**	**25**	**26**

Codeword 137

■	2	■	9	7	22	8	7	26	16	■	9	■
3	8	9	3 **A**	■	8	■	3	■	10	4	3	20
■	25	■	19	17	3	9	16	7	9	■	11	■
21	14	6	7	■	6	■	7	■	19	17	7	1
■	10	■	■	14	25	25	26	■	7	■	10	
19	9	3	21	■	15	■	■	3	15	3	9	
10	■	19	10	13	20	9	14	24	17	16	■	5
18	14	16	16	■	■	■	18	■	3	20	7	26
7	■	10	■	26	1	3	13	■	■	23	■	
16	3	9	25 **N**	■	9	■	9	■	19	6	7	15
■	19	■	3	23	10	6	10	16	6	■	18	■
26	25	3	13	■	25	■	12	■	10	10	13 **P**	26
■	7	■	26	8	24	24	7	26	16	■	16	■

A	B	C	D	E	F	G	H	I	J	K	L	M
N	O	P	Q	R	S	T	U	V	W	X	Y	Z

1	2	3	4	5	6	7	8	9	10	11	12	13
14	15	16	17	18	19	20	21	22	23	24	25	26

Codeword 138

	13	17	16	16	18	9	5		24	17	11	20
9		15		1		15			9		8	
23	25	17	2	18		11	26	17	19	9	17	25
25		18		20		1		16			4	
2	11	1	15		6	8	9	16	2 (I)	14	9	5
6		21		6		9		1		10		
	16	1	1	18	3		19	8	25	18	10	
		25		17		7		5		1		5
1	13	3	9	3	3	9	5		3	6	9	22
	17			12		15		2		26		9
3	20	10	22	17	8	5		3	11	1	22	18
	9		17			9		18		15 (N)		18 (L)
1	5	5	3		17	5	26	9	8	9	3	

A	B	C	D	E	F	G	H	I	J	K	L	M
N	O	P	Q	R	S	T	U	V	W	X	Y	Z

1	2	3	4	5	6	7	8	9	10	11	12	13
14	15	16	17	18	19	20	21	22	23	24	25	26

Codeword 139

The grid contains the following numbered cells:

		8		5		18		9		25		15
	3	20	4	3	20	9		24	7	17	23	7
		3		25		6	9	8		3		7
8	13	1	10	3	20			14	13	6	7	17
3			7			19		7		21		
20	7	23	7	20	18		21	12	25	7	24	
20		9			26	21	21			17		4
	10	3	13	21	16		18	11	16	3	17 R	7
	9		7		1					18		7
14	21	17	18	7		7	20	7	23	7	24
21		21		16	6	18		9		9 I	
3	12	25	7	17		3	5 D	23	9	8	7
2		9		21		22		7		7	

A B C D E F G H I J K L M
N O P Q R S T U V W X Y Z

1	2	3	4	5	6	7	8	9	10	11	12	13
14	15	16	17	18	19	20	21	22	23	24	25	26

Codeword 140

	1		2		10		19		25		8	
13	15	21	8	12	6		6	14	20	8	26	19
	6		4		12		23		8		15	
20	17 D	8	21		15	18	6	24	21	20	18	10
	15				6		1		15		19	
13	1	15	16	6	11	12	20	8	18	19		
	19		5						16		17	
	13	6	1	15	18	12	5	15	19	15	19	
	25		19		23		6				18	
4	6	19 S	12	15	23	11	21		6	22	20	18
	10 G		20		8		15		9		3	
10	11	20	12	6	1		18	6	11	19	15	6
	15		7		12		12		6		18	

A B C D E F G H I J K L M
N O P Q R S T U V W X Y Z

1	2	3	4	5	6	7	8	9	10	11	12	13
14	15	16	17	18	19	20	21	22	23	24	25	26

Codeword 141

	6	10	22	4	1	12	13			18	26	15	17
1		20		15		13				13		15	
3	1	4	1	17	4	14		6	1	26	10	15	
15		21		25		25		1		18		16	
4	15	14	7	18		13	24	24	13	4	20		
1				5		6		24		13		3	
26	10	5	1	20	13		23	10	26	26	5	13	
15		15 (O)		1		1		25				25	
	11	1	6	17	13	26		21	13	13	5	25	
9		26		4		19		17		8		13	
13	26	10	24	14		18	17	13	2	18	1	5	
25		17				25		25		26		25	
20	15	12	25		25	20	1	25	21	13	26		

A B C D E F G H I J K L M
N O P Q R S T U V W X Y Z

1	2	3	4	5	6	7	8	9	10	11	12	13
14	15	16	17	18	19	20	21	22	23	24	25	26

(Given letters: 15 = O, 22 = D, 13 = E)

Codeword 142

19	8	15	15	■	23	■	7	■	4	12	11	12
4	■	23	■	12	5	8	18	20	■	19		10
1	8	1	8	■	8	■	1	■	7	18	4	9
10	■	4	13	23	4	■	18	13	9	25	■	6
■	20	■	3 **G**	■	1	9	23	■	22	■	20	■
15	13	23	23	21	23	■	12	1	4	14	23	20
■	9	■	■	18	■	■	■	18	■	■	16	■
1	9	22	4	1	9	■	23	25	1	18	1	14
■	17	■	26	■	15	4	24	■	6	■	12	■
18	■	10	4	17	15	■	19	4	18	20		23
20 **D**	9 **O**	9	13	■	23	■	9	■	25	4	2	14
17	■	3	■	7	13	8	12	10	■	8		23
23	4	12	14	■	12	■	23	■	23	16	16	12

A	B	C	D	E	F	G	H	I	J	K	L	M
N	O	P	Q	R	S	T	U	V	W	X	Y	Z

1	2	3	4	5	6	7	8	9	10	11	12	13
14	15	16	17	18	19	20	21	22	23	24	25	26

Grid clues (numbers and given letters):

Row 1: 9, 25, 21, 4, 9/**P**, 13
Row 2: 4, 8, 6, 21, 25, 11, 11, 15, 18, 6, 14, 15
Row 3: 10, 8, 13, 6, 14, 11, 11
Row 4: 25, 6, 19, 10, 8, 10, 2, 10, 4, 11, 22
Row 5: 14, 6, 24, 3, 12
Row 6: 5, 8, 14, 6, 8, 11, 2, 8, 13, 2, 18
Row 7: 6, 10, 17, 6, 21, 18, 19
Row 8: 13, 11, 18, 24, 2, 18, 26, 18, 6, 2/**I**, 13
Row 9: 23, 1, 8, 16, 23
Row 10: 2, 3, 2, 25, 11, 18, 11, 20, 8, 10/**T**, 2
Row 11: 15, 11, 18, 2, 6, 11, 2
Row 12: 13, 2, 7, 22, 2, 18, 5, 11, 5, 2, 14, 10
Row 13: 14, 21, 3, 9, 16, 10

Letter key:

A B C D E F G H I J K L M
N O P Q R S T U V W X Y Z

1	2	3	4	5	6	7	8	9	10	11	12	13

14	15	16	17	18	19	20	21	22	23	24	25	26

Codeword 144

18	7	3	23	7		4	11	7	12	12	7	12
	3		25		18		26		3		15	
10	13	24	21	21	24	18	25		18	7	7	12
	5		7		21		23		12		21	
16	8	3	13	9	3		7	1	3	21	5	
			24		18		13				7	
23	3	13	2		25	26	12		19	25	16	7
	21				17		25		8			
	6	11	24	5	3		5	13	25	21	20	2
	11		5		5		25		12		24	
14	25	26	5		25	16 (D)	7	26	5	25	22	2
	13		7		24		12		18		5	
19	7	3	13	25 (I)	26	4		9 (M)	7	5	3	18

A B C D E F G H I J K L M
N O P Q R S T U V W X Y Z

1	2	3	4	5	6	7	8	9	10	11	12	13
14	15	16	17	18	19	20	21	22	23	24	25	26

Codeword 145

	16		19		26		24		21		7
	25	15	16	15	6	5		1	26	4	6	23
		15		5		25	13	4		16		15
3	5	12	25	1	16			6	7	25	5	22
17 **L**			16				9		5		4	
5	17	19	4	26	7		4	26	11	15	20	
10		7			26	4	19			12		1
	6	5 **A**	6	6	23		15	26	14	7	23	16
	5		7		18				7			15
10	20	5	21	26			19	1 **U**	6	6	15	20
7		19		15	26	10		20		20		
6	13	15	6	5		20	5	26	2	15	10	
15		6		6		23		16		8		

A	B	C	D	E	F	G	H	I	J	K	L	M
N	O	P	Q	R	S	T	U	V	W	X	Y	Z

1	2	3	4	5	6	7	8	9	10	11	12	13
14	15	16	17	18	19	20	21	22	23	24	25	26

Codeword 146

	21	16	3	15	18	21	16		2	19	26	25
9		14		25		16			1		11 **D**	
25	26	20	18	7		26	13	13	25	26	18	5
26		16		26		4		26			16	
11	15	7	8		11	2 **O**	15	9	20	10	15	25
16		4		17		7		25		26		
	25	18	19	16	4		24	16	20	13	17	
		19		21		2		4		20		18
13	25	16	26	7	16	21	4		23	2	6	4
	2			18		26		4		21		25
2	19	16	21	26	25	25		12 **P**	21	18	22	16
	16		26			25		16		16		4
20	21	2	11		16	6	16	1	26	4	17	

A	B	C	D	E	F	G	H	I	J	K	L	M
N	O	P	Q	R	S	T	U	V	W	X	Y	Z

1	2	3	4	5	6	7	8	9	10	11	12	13
14	15	16	17	18	19	20	21	22	23	24	25	26

Codeword 147

	14		17		22		24		16	
14 **P**	23	17	25	8		13	17	22	3	8	1
17		23		1		13		18		17		17
22	18	6	17	23	2	8		1	22	15	5	8
19		6		5		17		2				12
8	8	5	25		8		17	8	13	18	25	8
9		8		22	7	1	8	17		1		12
6	20	17	22	1	8		16		25 **S**	5	23	15
26				8		25		14		26		8
1	24	5	22	1		10	18	26	9	11	8	17
2		22		8		18		4		8		8
	13	26	8	25	6	23		26	21	5	8	21 **D**
		1		25		21		8		24		

A B C D E F G H I J K L M
N O P Q R S T U V W X Y Z

1	2	3	4	5	6	7	8	9	10	11	12	13
14	15	16	17	18	19	20	21	22	23	24	25	26

Codeword 148

6	2	26	3		12		7		11	3	14	10
2		14		11	24	18	22	6		8		2
6	15	14	4		18		1		14	22	15	20
12		23	14 **O**	4	22		1	12	8	14		11
	9		25		7	12	2		4		19	
21	12	8	11	18	11		11	3	2	3	12	5
	25			8				2			10	
5	14	17	22	25	14		4	18	8	21	12	11
	25		8		6	2	2		18		15	
3		5	22	12	3		18	13 **G**	15	20		12
2	13	12	11		2		13		12	2	3 **T**	11
15		10		23	22	13	26	3		10		7
16	12	20	11		25		3		22	25	16	20

A	B	C	D	E	F	G	H	I	J	K	L	M
N	O	P	Q	R	S	T	U	V	W	X	Y	Z

1	2	3	4	5	6	7	8	9	10	11	12	13
14	15	16	17	18	19	20	21	22	23	24	25	26

Codeword 149

21	26	19	6	8	26	19	■	11	23	21	19	23
■	21	■	20	■	13 **I**	■	3	■	11	■	16	■
23	4	1	23	8	1	21	13	4	25 **M**	23	4	1
■	4	■	8	■	23	■	24	■	■	■	1	■
14	23	16	22	6	8	9	19	■	5	12	21	1
■	9	■	12	■	■	■	21	■	6	■	2	■
■	8 **R**	23	20	13	23	22	13	4	24	■	■	
■	5	■	11	■	1	■	■	■	7	■	19	■
7	13	8	25	■	21	9	23	10	15	21	1	23
■	1	■	■	■	11	■	8	■	19	■	21	■
6	8	24	21	4	13	18	21	1	13	6	4	19
■	13	■	12	■	5	■	19	■	6	■	5	■
19	5	8	21	17	■	17	23	4	4	13	23	19

A B C D E F G H I J K L M
N O P Q R S T U V W X Y Z

1	2	3	4	5	6	7	8	9	10	11	12	13
14	15	16	17	18	19	20	21	22	23	24	25	26

Codeword 150

	17	18	21			22	10	10 **E**		26	
	13		14	6	10	4		19	18	5	19
21	23	14 **I**	13			23	5	13 **T**		4	
	14		7	8	11	19		10	25	14	12
4	24	10	6		4			23		12	4	8
5			23	4	2		4	17	1		17	
1	4	25	4		18	7	11		19	18	13	10
	3		21	4	23		4	16	18			25
20	12	5		9			15		9	18	11	10
	10	24	14	9		12	10	10	1		10	
		10		5	17	10			14	18	19	17
	18	19	5	17		4	11	10	19		6	
		6		10	10	1			16	4	17	

A	B	C	D	E	F	G	H	I	J	K	L	M
N	O	P	Q	R	S	T	U	V	W	X	Y	Z

1	2	3	4	5	6	7	8	9	10	11	12	13
14	15	16	17	18	19	20	21	22	23	24	25	26

Codeword 151

	19	12	24	23	18	9	20		26	11	11	23
8		11		8		12			15		22	
12	18	14	20 **T**	6		8	16	8	7	11	8	14 **S**
15		19		14		20		14			7	
14	4	11	13		12	11	21	7	11	9	20	14
11		9		5		12		11		24		
	14	20	11	8	3		13	11	11	26	6	
		11		12		9		19		20		4
18	26	23 **D**	11	12	7	15	11		25	15	5	11
	11			11		12		10		26		11
20	15	20	8	26	15	9		11	1	18	15	19
	10		3			7		26		8		14
9	2	24	19		12	11	17	11	8	7	14	

A B C D E F G H I J K L M
N O P Q R S T U V W X Y Z

1	2	3	4	5	6	7	8	9	10	11	12	13
14	15	16	17	18	19	20	21	22	23	24	25	26

Codeword 152

13 **A**	26	26	22	11	18			18		1	25	19
	22		4		13		18	9	13	9		22
16	13	5	3	22	23	18		1		2	21	23
	8 **U**			17		22	15	8			4	
22	6	22	5	8	23	22		26	2	10	8	18
13		23		13		12			14		23	
1	22	13	4	4	11		13	15	13	20	22	18
	12		25			5		25		2		3
14	25	24	22	1		9	25	18	23	2	1	11
	5			22	19	2		23			13	
13	23	22		23		7	13	18	23	25	10	19
18		15	25	1	22		4		7		19	
24	1	2		2		24	9	2 **O**	10	22	12	

A	B	C	D	E	F	G	H	I	J	K	L	M
N	O	P	Q	R	S	T	U	V	W	X	Y	Z

1	2	3	4	5	6	7	8	9	10	11	12	13
14	15	16	17	18	19	20	21	22	23	24	25	26

Codeword 153

17	5	7	26	24	20		12	17	16	8	7	14
7		9		7		2		22		16		7
13	22	7	17	10 (T)	12	16	5	17		26	14	8
22		5		15		22		2		5		7
7	26	10		2	16	14	14	12	3	12	7	6
1				22		17				5		20
	2	7	1	11	17		23	7	12	18	2	
17 (S)		8				17		20				21
7	17	11	12	16	5	26	18 (G)	7		7	14	26
1		16		4		3		25		19		22
6	7	23		16	11	7	14	26	10	12	16	5
16		7		5		17		1		1		10
8	26	14	24	7	10		26	1	12	7	5	17

A B C D E F G H I J K L M
N O P Q R S T U V W X Y Z

1	2	3	4	5	6	7	8	9	10	11	12	13
14	15	16	17	18	19	20	21	22	23	24	25	26

Codeword 154

23	15	25	26	15	12		14	25	26	20	23	11
	8		20		26		1		19		1	
3	9	26	18		10	15	18	25	21	26	7	17
	19	**I**	9 **U**		15				25		7	
12	15	25	25	6	16		12	26	25	20	26	14
			11		6		26				7	
24	7	15	15		10	1	7		4	6	17	11
	6				24		26		6			
15	13	26	14	22	11		11	15 **E**	26	2	15	19
	15		26				5		7		10	
17	25	1	19	26	6	25	26		22	10	6	22
	22		15		19		7		25		19	
5	21	23	10	26	19		17	15	21	11	15	10

A	B	C	D	E	F	G	H	I	J	K	L	M
N	O	P	Q	R	S	T	U	V	W	X	Y	Z

1	2	3	4	5	6	7	8	9	10	11	12	13
14	15	16	17	18	19	20	21	22	23	24	25	26

Codeword 155

	11		2		1		5		23		4	
7	2	10	18	24	15		8	17	8	15	26	8
	4		18		8 **A**		15		1		16	
20	25	9	20		24	3 **N**	24	20	8	14	15	26
	26				20		26		4		10	
16 **P**	4	2	21	4	26	20	20	9	2	3		
	20		26						3		2	
		24	3	1	2	3	20	1	9	2	24	20
	8		26		4		9				19	
6	24	9	19	19	9	3	21		19	2	20	12
	4		9		26		12		26		9	
18	8	15	1	2	3		19	24	22	26	13	2
	15		20		19		20		19		26	

A	B	C	D	E	F	G	H	I	J	K	L	M
N	O	P	Q	R	S	T	U	V	W	X	Y	Z

1	2	3	4	5	6	7	8	9	10	11	12	13
14	15	16	17	18	19	20	21	22	23	24	25	26

	21	20	7	6	5	7	26		14	21	23	7
2		2		13		16				6		12
17	6	1	2	10	25	7		14	4	26 **D**	14	7
3		21		25		4		8		4		26
7	18	5	1	6		5	14	4	5	7	26	
13				14		21		2		21		24
5	7	13	15	4	2 **O**		7	1	6	21	7	1
21		2		5		6		6				7
	2	22	5	14	4	8		11	6	8	14	13
14		12		4 **N**		7		25		23		19
24	23	14	4	8		14	4	21	5	6	23	23
24		4				21		7		9		7
12	2	8	14		21	5	6	21	15	7	26	

A	B	C	D	E	F	G	H	I	J	K	L	M
N	O	P	Q	R	S	T	U	V	W	X	Y	Z

1	2	3	4	5	6	7	8	9	10	11	12	13
14	15	16	17	18	19	20	21	22	23	24	25	26

Codeword 157

2	15	6	17	3	20	■	■	25	■	19	8	4
■	6	■	6	■	7	■	26	8	18	20	■	25
21	2	20	16	25	20	15	■	22	■	11	6	10
■	22	■	■	5	■	1	9	25	■	■	23	■
5	6	17	3	20	6	2	■	1	9	6	25	22
6	■	7	■	14	■	13	■	■	25	■	8	■
10	16	20	6	15	7	■	25	22	1	8	14 (M)	20
■	20	■	9	■	■	17	■	6	■	6	■	24
8	15	1	6	16	■	8	17	15	20	16	12	20
■	20	■	■	25	3	3	■	6	■	■	25	■
15	5	7	■	15	■	13	20	3	6	7	20	13
2	■	20	12	20 (E)	16	■	10	■	25	■	24	■
22	20	5	■	15	■	■	8	3	13 (D)	20	15	5

A B C D E F G H I J K L M
N O P Q R S T U V W X Y Z

1	2	3	4	5	6	7	8	9	10	11	12	13
14	15	16	17	18	19	20	21	22	23	24	25	26

Codeword 158

		9		21		23		6		21		
26	10	16	11	20		7	19	23	13	20	21	
11		13		8		14		9		10		1
20	18	23	5	16	22 **N**	20		12	23	16	24	15
13		5		9		22		20				23
10 **L**	23	16	22		20		23	13	9	6	15	10
26		7		2	13	26	4	7		20		16
26	19	15	10	23	13		20		19	23	10	6
24				16		23		20		9		16
20	10	6	16	22		19	26	22	17	15	13 **R**	20
21		26		16		22		17		13		13
	8	13	26	22	25	20		26	8	20	3	7
		24		2		21		3		21		

A	B	C	D	E	F	G	H	I	J	K	L	M
N	O	P	Q	R	S	T	U	V	W	X	Y	Z

1	2	3	4	5	6	7	8	9	10	11	12	13
14	15	16	17	18	19	20	21	22	23	24	25	26

Codeword 159

24	4 (O)	10	16		3		5		22	8	11	22
19		14		14	25	1 (G)	22	14		11		19
26	25	22	14 (L)		20		20		3	19	25	3
25		12	19	2	19		2	15	19	16		24
	19		6		3	11	25		14		24	
11	15	24	22	10	25		16	22	14	2	19	25
	22			11				24			13	
25	15	16	19	6	25		24	23	25	25	16	24
	25		3		18	4	4		17		23	
22		1	14	4	17		6	19	17	24		11
24	12	22	9		25		16		24	19	16	24
21		7		22	3	3	25	6		10		25
24	11	25	24		24		3		24	16	11	3

A	B	C	D	E	F	G	H	I	J	K	L	M
N	O	P	Q	R	S	T	U	V	W	X	Y	Z

1	2	3	4	5	6	7	8	9	10	11	12	13
14	15	16	17	18	10	20	21	22	23	24	25	26

	11	13	8	1	13	10	17		8	26	17	13
17		18		8		13			11		9	
7	19	26	8	14		15	8	10	13	4	16	11
19		11		13		19 **O**		19			6	
26	10	19	2		1	6	17	7	16	10	24	17
17		1		8		11		8		13		
	2	6	23	1	12		17	7	8	7	13	
		23		20		17		13		10		16
17	16	22	22	13	17	7	17		5	6	22	17
	10			10		16		4		13		16
13	22	22	20	13	8	1		11	19	3	13	10
	13		8			6 **I**		13		8 **A**		26
8	17	21	17		25	19	10	8	11	11	12	

A	B	C	D	E	F	G	H	I	J	K	L	M
N	O	P	Q	R	S	T	U	V	W	X	Y	Z

1	2	3	4	5	6	7	8	9	10	11	12	13
14	15	16	17	18	19	20	21	22	23	24	25	26

Codeword 161

	1		10		24		3		7		16	
15	19	13 **E**	4	20	10		4	24	20	21	19	7
	13		19		18	17	17		13		9	
7	13	19	26 **M**	21	17		22		15	4	25	18
	2				4	16 **G**	21				16	
2	13	3	19	4		13		25	18	17	13	7
		21		8	13	17	17	12		4		
1	19	21	17	20		18		13	3	3	13	25
	13			23	13	20				14	
4	1	4	19		21		15	4	6	19	9	7
	6		13		18	24	13		13		4	
24	13	19	13	4	6		13	17	4	3	6	13
	5		11		4		25		17		7	

A B C D E F G H I J K L M
N O P Q R S T U V W X Y Z

1	2	3	4	5	6	7	8	9	10	11	12	13
14	15	16	17	18	19	20	21	22	23	24	25	26

Solutions

1

A C A Z K M
SQUASH ORATE
U L AGO N Z
CHASMS SKATE
R K L O E
EXPIRE AFIRE
W S DRY E E
AIMED SURVEY
S O Y E E
PHIAL JUDGED
O C OFF S O
DWEEB OPERAS
S D E P S L

2

ACQUITS ODDS
P O N E W R
ACNED AZALEAS
T T O P N F
CORK POLYMATH
H A B T W N
SCRAP PAUSE
T L S Y W S
ABSOLUTE TEXT
A O A J R O
PSALTER ADIEU
I E V I N T
ACED GEOLOGY

3

C T I P E B
WADING LUXURY
R P U A T I
ZIPS ASSORTED
B N M A F
NONCHALANCE
U O T R
EMBARRASSES
Y P L H J
VELOCITY LEEK
L S G M O C
SPEECH EQUATE
S S T D T S

4

BASHES CITRIC
I Q T A N E A
FLUSHES JOINT
F E E K U K E
GEAR EARLIER
S Z W E I
UNEVEN ASSIGN
B X B N G
SOMEONE ROVE
I E T E O O I
SUSHI COUPLES
T O C H N V L
SYNTAX ADHERE

5

D Q J S C M
MODULE PIZZAS
M A WAR A G
FIDDLE I RAPS
N LAG I
FOCUS W EXPEL
H ENACT R
OLIVE K AGONY
U PER A
BRIG H ALTERS
K R ORB E R
RESIGN BEACON
D M E I R W

6

ALKALI UNABLE
O P N N Q A
EWER DEFAULTS
E O E O A E
TRANSFER TORE
E A T I
ADJUST UNCLAD
T I N C
TAXI GRAPHICS
G L A T O U
VARIABLE ROSY
I T L L D E
ENZYME YIELDS

7

```
B I O S . S . Q . S T A B
O . Y . G A M U T . H . A
P E E L . F . O . B I T S
S . Z O N E . T O Y S . S
. C . N . S U E . T . S .
C A U G H T . D R E A M S
. R . E . . E . . O .
T R A I N S . E F F E C T
. Y . N . P E A . L . K .
H . O K R A . S W A G . G
E N V Y . C . I . K A L E
L . E . J E L L Y . R . N
M I N X . S . Y . A B L E
```

8

```
B R O W N . O U T S I D E
. E . A . Q . N . W . R .
T H E S A U R I . E X A M
. A . S . A . V . E . I .
O B T A I N . E A T E N .
. . I . T . R . . . E .
R E E L . I F S . B A D E
. J . Z . I . O . .
E X T R A . T R O O P S .
. C . E . T . I . K . A .
S T U N . I D E O L O G Y
. E . E . O . S . E . E .
E D I T I N G . S T A S H
```

9

```
. M . A . O . Q . J .
N A I L S . B R U T A L
O . L . C . E . A . Z . C
T R I L O G Y . R A Z O R
I . T . T . S . R . . I
C O A X . O . P E D A N T
E . N . O F F A L . L . I
A R T I S T . W . B L O C
B . . T . S . O . I . I
L O V E R . P I Z Z A Z Z
Y . E . I . A . O . N . E
. T R U C K S . N I C K S
. Y . H . M . E . E
```

10

```
. P . Y . S . S . S . I
G A L O S H . H U M A N S
. N . G . A I R . U . R
W I Z A R D . U . G O U T
. N . . E B B . . . S
F I N E S . I . P A T H S
. . E . H I N T S . A
Q U E R Y . D . I N D E X
. P . . V I D . . . J
A S P S . O . R E N D E R
. I . K . W O O . E . C
A D V I C E . W E A L T H
. E . S . L . N . T . S
```

11

```
I C I C L E . Q . Z A G
. O . A . T . J U D O . E
O V E R L A P . E . O D E
. E . . E . U P S . . I
P R O T E I N . T E X T S
A . A . R . K . G . T
R E F U S E . P H O T O S
. A . S . H . A . W . U
G R I E F . U N I F O R M
. T . . A P E . R . . E
W H Y . U . S O Y B E A N
R . I D L E . N . I . D
Y E N . T . . E M B R Y O
```

12

```
B . W . M . C . B . H . H
A S O C I A L . O P E R A
N . R . R . E . G . I . N
J O K E R . F I G U R E D
O . S . O . . . L . . . L
. C H A R A C T E R I Z E
B . O . . O . . . N . S .
E X P L O I T A T I V E .
D . . B . . . A . A . B
R E Q U E S T . R O D E O
O . U . Y . I . I . I . O
O V A T E . D E F I N E S
M . Y . D . E . F . G . T
```

13

14

15

16

17

18

19

```
A F F O R D   S T E R E O
J U   I   U   O   A   V
A C C U S E D   P R I Z E
R   H   E   D   S   N   R
  U S E S   E X P O S E S
A   I   R   I       E
N E A R B Y   A N G O R A
Y   R   R       P   S
W E L C O M E   A G A R
H   O   T   P   G   Q   I
E P O C H   A I R G U N S
R   K   E   Y   E   E   L
E N S U R E   D E G R E E
```

20

```
  V I A   H I C   T
  O   V I L E   L I O N
P I N E   C H I   X
L   R A C K   Q U I P
M A W S   R   U   C A P
U   I C E   J E T   W
G Y R O   E V E   E A S Y
E   N A P   W A R   A
F A D   V   E   R A M P
  H O B O   P L E A   E
  Z   I R E   P Y R E
W E L D   A N T I   I
  N   S I R   N U T
```

21

```
  M   T   R   Z   M   G
  P E S E T A   E X I L E
  N   A   J U T   D   N
S Q U A R E     A F I R E
O   S     B   I   A
B O T H E R   E A R L Y
S   A     A H A   A   T
  O R B I T   M E M B E R
  W   E   S     A   U
C L O T H     I N C O M E
A   V   U R N   U   K
S M A L L   U N L O A D
H   L   L   N   L   Y
```

22

```
S   D   D   A   M   F   F
Q U O T I N G   I C I E R
U   W   S   E   L   Z   E
I O N I C   D R I Z Z L E
B   P   U   E       I
  C O N S T I T U T I O N
S   U   F       N   G
C I R C U M S T A N C E
I   N     D   L   C
E N J O Y E D   V O U C H
N   E   O   I   I   D   O
C L E R K   E X C E E D S
E   R   E   D   E   D   E
```

23

```
T O P A Z   D I S P O S E
Z   B   P   N   R   Q
S O M E W H A T   O P U S
N   T   O   R   O   A
S E X T E T   O F F E R
  E   O   D       E
G I L D   G N U   B A S K
N   R   C   E
  J U N T A   T W E L V E
U   O   P   O   S   E
I R O N   H A R D W A R E
E   E   E   Y   A   S
E D I T O R S   E X P E L
```

24

```
  S   J   C   V   Z   G
D E T A C H   A P A T H Y
  Q   I   I L L   N   E
M U S L I N   V   Y E T I
  E     A P E     T
G L E A M   A   A R G O N
  R   A B Y S S   A
A R R O W   E   K I L L S
  A     R E F     O
G N A T   E   L I N E A R
  G   E   L E I   A   D
H E R N I A   N O I S E S
  D   T   X   G   L   D
```

Solutions

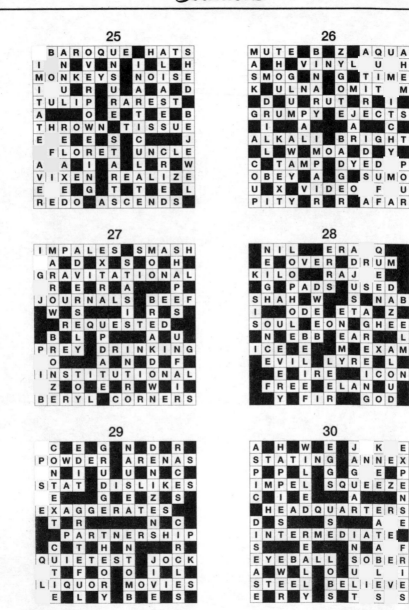

25

	B	A	R	O	Q	U	E		H	A	T	S
I		N		V		N			I		L		H
M	O	N	K	E	Y	S		N	O	I	S	E
I		U		R		U		A		A		D
T	U	L	I	P		R	A	R	E	S	T	
A			O		E		T		E		B
T	H	R	O	W	N		T	I	S	S	U	E
E		E		E		S		C			J
	F	L	O	R	E	T		U	N	C	L	E
A		A		I		A		L		R		W
V	I	X	E	N		R	E	A	L	I	Z	E
E		E		G		T		T		E		L
R	E	D	O		A	S	C	E	N	D	S	

26

| M | U | T | E | | B | | Z | | A | Q | U | A |
|A| |H| |V|I|N|Y|L| |U| |H|
|S|M|O|G| |N| |G| |T|I|M|E|
|K| |U|L|N|A| |O|M|I|T| |M|
	D		U		R	U	T		R		I	
G	R	U	M	P	Y		E	J	E	C	T	S
	I		A		A		A			C	
A	L	K	A	L	I		B	R	I	G	H	T
	L		W		M	O	A		D		Y	
C		T	A	M	P		D	Y	E	D		P
O	B	E	Y		A		G		S	U	M	O
U		X		V	I	D	E	O		F		U
P	I	T	Y		R		R		A	F	A	R

27

| I | M | P | A | L | E | S | | S | M | A | S | H |
|A| |D| |X| |S| |O| |H|
G	R	A	V	I	T	A	T	I	O	N	A	L
R		E		R		A			P
J	O	U	R	N	A	L	S		B	E	E	F
W		S		I		R		S
	R	E	Q	U	E	S	T	E	D	
B		L		P		A		U
P	R	E	Y		D	R	I	N	K	I	N	G
O		A		N		D		F
I	N	S	T	I	T	U	T	I	O	N	A	L
Z		O		E		R		W		I
B	E	R	Y	L		C	O	R	N	E	R	S

28

	N	I	L		E	R	A		Q	
	E		O	V	E	R		D	R	U	M
K	I	L	O		R	A	J		E
G		P	A	D	S		U	S	E	D
S	H	A	H		W		S		N	A	B
I		O	D	E		E	T	A		Z
S	O	U	L		E	O	N		G	H	E	E
N		E	B	B		E	A	R		L
I	C	E		E		M		E	X	A	M
	E	V	I	L		L	Y	R	E		L
	E		I	R	E		I	C	O	N
F	R	E	E		E	L	A	N		U
	Y		F	I	R		G	O	D

29

| | C | | E | | G | | N | | D | | R | |
|P|O|W|D|E|R| |A|R|E|N|A|S|
|N| |I| |U| |U| |N| |C|
|S|T|A|T| |D|I|S|L|I|K|E|S|
|E| |G| |E| |Z| |S|
E	X	A	G	G	E	R	A	T	E	S	
	T		R			N		C
	P	A	R	T	N	E	R	S	H	I	P
	C		T		H		N		R
Q	U	I	E	T	E	S	T		J	O	C	K
	T		F		O		O		I		L
L	I	Q	U	O	R		M	O	V	I	E	S
	E		L		Y		B		E		S

30

| A | H | W | E | | J | | K | | E |
|S|T|A|T|I|N|G| |A|N|N|E|X|
|P| |P| |L| |G| |G| |E| |P|
I	M	P	E	L		S	Q	U	E	E	Z	E
C		I		E		A			N
	H	E	A	D	Q	U	A	R	T	E	R	S
D		S		S		S			A		E
I	N	T	E	R	M	E	D	I	A	T	E	
S		E			E		N		A		F
E	Y	E	B	A	L	L		S	O	B	E	R
A		W		L		O		U		L		I
S	T	E	E	L		B	E	L	I	E	V	E
E		R		Y		S		T		S	S

31

```
. H J T . Q U . I .
V A N I S H . U P S I D E
. I . B . R Y E . E . I .
B R E E Z E . R . S H O W
. D . . W R Y . A . . T .
L O T T O . A . G R O S S
. . A . F A B L E . A . .
G R U F F . B . N A K E D
. E . . . V I D . . N . .
I S L E . O . A B L A Z E
. E . X . T O R . O . Y .
A T T I R E . E N C A M P
. S . T . R . D . O . E .
```

32

```
. N F A . L U . E
F O O L E D . A L D E R
. D . O . S U M . O . G
R I S K E D . B A N J O
O . O . . Z . S . A .
B A S I N G . O T H E R
E . U . U R N . R . A
. D E C A Y . E X T R A S
U . U . S . . O . P
V O W E L . A L W A Y S
A . I . U P S . O . N
S A F E S . E Q U A T E
T . E . H T . D . S
```

33

```
. P . E Y E W A S H . A .
R A P T . Q . X . I L L S
. N . C O U R I E R . S .
W I S H . A . O . E G O S
. N . . T A M E . O . L .
F I L E . O . . S O D A
E . O V E R L O O K S . S
T U B E . U . Y E A H
E . B . S L O T . . M .
D A Y S . A . S . P E A K
. R . H O S T I L E . Z .
M I N I . S . D . L E E S
. A . P R O J E C T . S .
```

34

```
S Q U A S H . T H R O W N
. U . C . I . E . E . A .
H I G H . E L E P H A N T
. T . I . R . . A . T .
P E S E T A . F A B R I C
. . V . R . I . . N .
M E M E . C A N . J U G S
X . . H . A . A .
S P O O K Y . L U M B A R
E . O . . I . M . D .
S C H M A L T Z . I D O L
T . P . E . E . N . P .
A S T H M A . S I G H T S
```

35

```
S T R E S S . . F . R I M
. H . M . I . F E T A . A
R E Q U E S T . L . J A Y
. T . B . A W L . . M .
M A I L B O X . A R R A Y
U . L . E . I . . E . Z
M E L O D Y . C O F F E E
. A . D . K . F . A . W
A S K E D . A F F A B L E
. E . . R E V . A . I .
E L K . Y . A P L E N T Y
O . E R A S . A . E . H
N A G . D . W A L L E T
```

36

```
R O D S . B . T . A B U T
I . E . D R E A D . U . E
G A L A . O . N . C R U X
S . I N F O . D E A R . T
. J . T . D Y E . R . B
M O D I F Y . M O S Q U E
I . E . . E . W . . S .
U S A G E S . A L I G H T
. T . A . A R C . D . Y
S . A V I D . C A L F . A
L O B E . D . E . Y A W S
A . E . T E M P T . Z . K
P A T H . N . T . L E S S
```

37

```
  Z L M   Z T   G
  B I K I N I   E Q U A L
  N   A   C U R   N   E
E N C O R E     O V A T E
C   I     J   I   A
H O L L O W   O D D E R
O   E   I N K     T   M
  P I N T S   E S C A P E
  R   A   E       O   M
H O B B Y   T U X E D O
O   Y   U P S   R   G
O P T I C   E N G A G E
F   E   K   W   E   Y
```

38

```
  S H A P I N G   U S E R
W   Y   E   O   R   T   E
E X P O R T S   E L A T E
B   E   S   H H   R   K
S T R I P   E X A L T S
I   E   S   B   L   M
T O P I C S   C I N E M A
E   I   T   A   L   A E
  E T H I C S   I O T A S
Z   F   V   H   T   R   T
E V A D E   O P A Q U E R
S   L   S   R   T   S   O
T A L E   R E J E C T S
```

39

```
  S C H O L A R   D E E R
S   L   R   S   I   X
K N I F E   L O B E L I A
I   M   S   E   O   S
R O A D   R E Q U E S T S
T   C   H   P   N   U
  S T O U T   A D O B E
  I   M   U   S   S   U
N E C K B A N D   J I G S
  A   U   I   L   D   A
B R O U G H T   O W I N G
  L   S   E   C   Z   E
T Y P E   A D V I S E S
```

40

```
M U E S L I   C I C A D A
  S   I   N   A   R   I
P U T T   A P P R O V E D
  A   U   B   W   H
A L K A L I   S Y N T A X
  T   L   P   R
M E Z E   I R E   M O D E
  Q   T   C   A
H U G E L Y   I N J E C T
  A   L   F   O   A
G L A D I O L I   R I B S
  L   E   L   E   L   I
H Y B R I D   S A Y I N G
```

41

```
J O W L   E   C   I T E M
U   A   S Q U A D   E   I
S A S H   U   L   T E R N
T   P A P A   I C O N   K
  G   L   L O P   U   F
F L O O D S   H A R D L Y
  A   U     S   E
A Z A L E A   C H O S E N
  E   O   B I O   V   T
S   W A D I   R E E F   A
C Y A N   D   R   R I O T
U   R   R E L A X   S   O
D U D S   S   L   S T E M
```

42

```
    A   D   F   A   W   S
  E X P I R E   Q U I C K
    L   E   E M U   R   I
E J E C T S     A B Y S S
L   O     C   A   I
M A S S I F   U T T E R
S   H   O A T   O   A
  T Y I N G   E V E N E D
  W   C   S   B   D
N O T E D   R O B O T S
A   R   O R C   U   I
B L I T Z   A B S E N T
S   M   E   Y   T   K
```

Solutions

43

44

45

46

47

48

49

```
C O M E D Y . S Q U A S H
L A . I . F U . F . O
I N J U S T I C E . F U N
M O . A . N S . R . E
A I R . V A C A T I O N S
X . . O H . . N . T
. S P A W N . M A T T E .
F A . . S . P . . . E
I N D I C A T O R . S O N
S D . A . A . I . A . Z
C H I . B A S I C A L L Y
A . N . I . H . O . V . M
L E G E N D . S T R O K E
```

50

```
. R A B . Q . A . E
G O S P E L . U R G E N T
. C . S . I C E . E . D
D O Z E N S . R . S W I M
. C . . . S T Y . . N
C O R G I . O . A D A G E
. . E . V O W E L . R .
H E F T Y . E . L I K E D
. S . . . E L F . . . R
S C A R . N . I N J U R E
. A . U . T A X . E . A
S P I D E R . E X T A N T
. E . D . Y . D . S . D
```

51

```
G E N T L E . T . L U G
. N . E . E . J O K E . A
U S U A L L Y . P . I F S
. U . . Y . E T A . . O
R E P L I C A . Z E B R A
O . E . N . H . G . M
E N R A G E . G L O S S Y
. A . C . S . O . K . E
M I L E S . T O A D I E S
. V . P R O . D . . Q
R E D . E . W A S H T U B
I . I M A M . Y . I . I
B O P . K . E X C E P T
```

52

```
. P O D . J U G . F
R . R H E A . L O O K
T O G A . D O E . C
S . W A G E . A Q U A
V E R B . O . N . S I P
E . . A D O . A S K . D
T O R C . E L M . A L S O
. D . K E Y . E O N . . F
Y E T . N . N . G A F F
. S E E R . I D E A . R
. X . O R C . . R O O F
S T U B . E U R O . Z
. S . E N D . O N E
```

53

```
P E S T . L . B . P R E P
A P . V I X E N . I . E
S C A B . Q . G . F A M E
. M E N U . I D O L . L
. J . A . O W N . C . F
J A G U A R . S K I L L S
. Z . L . . O . . I
A Z A L E A . F I S H E D
. Y . I . P H I . A . S
P . E V I L . D E W Y . W
L Y R E . O . G . S E M I
O . A . U M B E R . L . M
P O S E . B . T . S L I P
```

54

```
R O B U S T . Y E A R N S
O . R . W . A . X . A Q
L O A D I N G . A D I E U
E . V . M . A . M . L E
. O A K S . I M P A S S E
F . D . . N . L . . . Z
I R O N E D . S E D A T E
G . . J . A . . . C . D
H A R D E N S . G R A B
T . O . C . I . A . D S
I N G O T . D A M P E S T
N . U . E . E . U . M U
G R E E D Y . S T A Y E D
```

55

```
. A S O C I A L . R O B S
V . O . O . S . . P . P .
A P L E N T Y . A M A Z E
C . A . T . L . U . Q . D
A I R E R . U N T R U E .
N . I . M . O . E . R . .
C L I M B S . E M E R G E
Y . N . U . T . O . . V .
. A V A T A R . B R A K E
A . O . O . I . I . L . R
J O K E R . F E L L O W S
A . E . . L . E . H . E .
R A S P . B E E S W A X .
```

56

```
. W . A I . F . P . S .
J A R G O N . E R E C T
. I . A . S O T . S . A
O F F E R S . A G O N Y
V . T . . . B . N . I .
E X P A N D . E Q U A L
N . O . A I D . I . M .
. A P P L Y . S H E L V E
S . E . S . . L . . T .
C H I C K . E F F A C E
O . D . I M P . L . Y .
B E L O W . A M A Z E D
S . E . I . P . N . S .
```

57

```
. R . C . O . F . A . H .
H E R O I C . I N B R E D
. Q . P . C . A . S . E .
D U L Y . U N S E T T L E
I . . R . C . R . S . . .
C R A F T S W O M A N . .
. E . O . . . C . E . . .
. P R O S P E C T I V E .
. T . E . E . A . . E . .
Y A C H T I N G . J U N K
. X . E . Z . L . U . I .
D E C A D E . E R M I N E
. S . D . D . S . P . G .
```

58

```
. M . D I S G U S T . V .
Z E R O . Q . N . I B I S
. T . C A U T I O N . N .
T R E K . E . O . S T E W
. I . . E O N S . H . I .
E C H O . Z . . D I E D .
X . A F T E R N O O N . O
P U T T . . E . . S K E W
E . E . E D G E . . . J .
L A D Y . W . D . S E E S
. T . O V E R L A P . C .
M O O R . E . E . R O T E
P . E M B A S S Y . S . .
```

59

```
E S T A T E . E Q U A T E
A . I . R . D . U . T . X
S U M M A R I Z E . T O P
I . I . I . S . E . E . O
N O D . N I C K N A M E S
G . . E . O . . . P . E .
. A B O R T . A G A T E .
E . A . . A . N . . . E .
M A N I F E S T O . J A R
B . A . L . S . C . U . A
R U N . O V E R C O M E S
Y . A . W . T . H . P . E
O B S E S S . B I A S E D
```

60

```
Z E S T . E . R . A Q U A
O . L . E X C E L . U . P
N A I L . P . I . W A G S
E . M I N I . G O A D . E
. I . M . R A N . L . O .
S T U B B Y . S P L I T S
C . . I . . . A . . H . .
G H E T T O . B L A M E S
. Y . W . F L U . R . R .
A . B I F F . R A C K . S
S L O T . I . E . H A C K
K . O . O C E A N . V . I
S E T S . E . U . J A W S
```

61

62

63

64

65

66

67

```
. N S . A . T M . H .
B E L I E F . A V A T A R
. T . G . F . T . H . S
S W A N . E X T R A C T S
. O . . . C . O . R . Y
G R A D A T I O N A L .
. K . E . . . . J . F
. U N D E S I R A B L E
. C . I . X . N . . O
P U Z Z L I N G . P E R K
. R . E . T . E . L . I
A V E N U E . S Q U A S H
. E . S . D . T . S . T
```

68

```
R I P E . E . L . O G L E
O . A . B L O O D . U . N
W A T T . I . I . T R O D
S . H O A X . T H O U . S
. M . F . I R E . G . M
L I Q U O R . R E A S O N
. N . N . . M . . I
G U I N E A . F U T U R E
. S . O . C H I . U . E
A . S U I T . N A B S . A
J O I N . I . G . S W A Y
A . Z . L O V E R . U . E
R E E K . N . R . I M P S
```

69

```
S C A R F . R E Q U E S T
. L . A . U . X . M . Q
D I S T I N C T . B L U R
. M . T . M . R . R . E
A B E L I A . A W A K E
. E . N . V . . . Z
S P E D . A H A . S E E D
. A . . G . G . U
. S E I Z E . A C R O S S
. S . N . A . N . V . H
G A G A . B A C H E L O R
. G . N . L . E . Y . N
B E J E W E L . A S K E W
```

70

```
G . B . F . S . S . J . P
R E A L I Z E . H O O K S
A . N . N . M . A . K . A
P U K K A . I N K W E L L
E . R . L . . E . . T
. Q U E S T I O N A B L E
M . P . L . . L . O . R
A R T I C U L A T I N G .
N . L . . H . E . A
A P P L I E S . E T H I C
G . U . M . A . O . E . U
E X T R A . V A R I A N T
R . S . X . E . Y . D . E
```

71

```
. W V . A . T . J . H
. B I K I N I . A L I B I
. S . S . L A X . B . N
R E P E A T . I N E P T
O . E . . Z . I . A
P I L L O W . E L B O W
Y . E . E T A . R . A
. F I G H T . L U M B A R
L . U . S . . U . E
Q U I T E . F A M O U S
U . C . A M P . P . U
A V O W S . A V E R S E
Y . N . E . L . D . T
```

72

```
. A B O L I S H . L O B S
A . O . O . E . . E . A
F A R M S . Q U O T I N G
I . R . E . U . U . . J
R O O D . T E X T B O O K
E . W . C . L . L . V
. T I A R A . N A K E D .
. N . U . A . W . R . P
O R G A N I Z E . A N T I
. A . C . A . T . I . L
A L C O H O L . A N G E L
. L . L . . E . R . H . S
D Y E D . C A V O R T S
```

73

74

75

76

77

78

79

```
C A R B S . E D I T I N G
. R . A . E . I . O . A .
P R E F I X E S . P O T S
. O . F . P . C . A . U .
T W E L V E . R A Z O R .
. E . C . I . . . A . . .
P A T S . T O M . H U L K
. C . A . I . I . . . . .
Q U E S T . N E S T E D .
. U . A . I . A . T . V .
J I G S . O U T C O M E S
. T . E . N . E . R . N .
U S E L E S S . C Y S T S
```

80

```
S M O K E D . P . Z I G .
. O . O . Y . B R I O . O
C R U I S E R . O . O L D
. A . O . E G O . . A . .
A L G E B R A . F E E D S
D . N . E . P . T . L . .
S Q U A R E . H E A T E D
. U . D . V . M . E . U .
M A J O R . E X P L A I N
. C . E A T . T . N . N .
S K Y . N . S O Y B E A N
K . U S E D . A . Y . P .
A I M . W . . T W E N T Y
```

81

```
J . M . M . A . G . S . G
O P A Q U E R . A M I G O
K . C . E . I . T . N . O
E T H O S . A V E N G E D
R . I . L . . A . . . . B
. I N D I V I D U A L L Y
S . E . R . . . A . E . .
U N S U C C E S S F U L .
C . . H . . . K . N . B .
C O N T E X T . I N C U R
E . A . W . O . N . H . A
S E I Z E . W A N D E R S
S . L . D . S . Y . D . S
```

82

```
A . N . L . . P . H . . V
S H E R I F F . O Z O N E
S . A . N . R . P . M . S
E R R . E Q U I P M E N T
M . . A . S . E . W . . .
B I T E R . T E D I O U S
L . R . . . . R . R . . I
E X O T I C A . J O K E D
. . U . N . T . O . . . E
A M B I G U I T Y . B O W
I . L . E . O . F . A . A
D E E M S . N A U G H T Y
S . S . T . . L . T . . S
```

83

```
. A . V . R . C . T . R .
. A L P A C A . O V A T E
. T . N . J A M . X . F .
C L O S E R . . A M I S S
O . P . . . H . I . O . .
B A N A N A . A S C O T .
S . E . N E W . . W . H .
. R E T R O . K I D N E Y
. E . E . N . . O . . P .
E V E N S . M O S Q U E .
X . V . L A W . Y . U . .
A D I E U . O P E R A S .
M . L . G . W . Z . D . .
```

84

```
. N . F . F . V . A . A .
A E R I A L . E Q U A L S
. U . Z . I O N . R . K .
F R O Z E N . O . A J A R
. A . . . G Y M . . L . .
C L I M B . U . A V O I D
. . L . R A C K S . F . .
C E L L O . C . K O F T A
. X . . . S A C . . A . .
P I T S . W . O B J E C T
. S . K . E M U . O . K .
S T R I K E . C A L L E D
. S . P . T . H . T . D .
```

85

Grid 85 solution with words including: H A O S P K, BELIEF AZALEA, X D F C R M, JADE SCHNAPPS, G E E N T, WORKSTATION, N N I S, CONCEIVABLY, Q C H R U, RUCKSACK OMIT, A I I I A C, WINNER NURSES, L G S G S S

86

Grid 86 solution with words including: EXPIRY STRING, N O A R N R, ALL INFLUENCE, M I L R N A, EATS WELCOMES, L I U Q A O Y, CONDUCTOR, A A L E E T I, BILLIONS VAIN, L K C J L T, ARCHETYPE IRE, Z O L S T N, ESSAYS STAYED

87

Grid 87 solution with words including: WORSHIP ASKS, S W T O Q O, TANKARD EQUAL, U E K I X E O, FARCE NUCLEI, F H E E Z S, EMPLOY UPKEEP, D R L A T R, VOIDED IMBUE, U J E D O O A, SWEAR IGNORED, E C N A E S, SITE AGELESS

88

Grid 88 solution with words including: B B T V W L, CAMERA IVORY, N T T UPS L N, MADCAP AFFIX, O O Q E M, PAGODA UNZIP, E O SEA F D, FORTH YEASTY, E E Y G E, BEEFY BLOCKS, I R ASP I U, THROW EJECTS, S S S C S E

89

Grid 89 solution with words including: FIDGET AVERSE, U E S A E U V, REFUSES NURSE, Y A A K T A R, RUBY EQUALLY, S L W R O, OUTPUT REJOIN, L P S D E, DELIGHT KEYS, I A R O N S E, EXTRA CROSSED, R E D K W E G, SERIES ENZYME

90

Grid 90 solution with words including: J H T F O S, BUREAU REFLEX, N R TEE F Q, DIRECT A SOUP, O I L K E, CRAZE A AMPLE, D VERBS H, STONE V HAIRY, U BAA E, ANTE L WRONGS, I C OVA N I, ANYHOW SALAMI, G O S H Y E

91

92

93

94

95

96

Solutions

97

98

99

100

101

102

103

```
. B . F . Z . S . T . A
P U M I C E . L I A B L E
. R . N . B E E . N . K .
V E N D O R . E . S L A B
. A . . A S P . . . L . .
Y U C C A . K . O R B I T
. . H . R O U G H . O . .
Q U I C K . L . M I X E S
. N . . E L F . . . J . .
U L N A . M . L A R G E R
. E . M . E W E . E . C .
I S O M E R . E X A L T S
. S . O . Y . T . R . S .
```

104

```
B U Z Z . S . R . I B I S
U . O . R E P E L . A . I
C O O P . Q . I . P H A T
K . M E N U . G O A T . E
. O . E . E O N . T . I .
J A C K A L . S P H E R E
. S . H . . . S . . K . .
K I D N A P . B I A S E D
. S . E . E M U . L . D .
L . N O V A . D O L T . D
O X E N . N . G . Y O K E
A . W . C U R E S . F . F
N O S Y . T . T . I F F Y
```

105

```
. C H E A P E R . R A S H
A . A . D . A . Q . N . I
B E C O M E S . U N T I L
O . K . I . I . A . E . T
R I S E N . L I N I N G .
T . . . Y . T . N . . . A
E X P O S E . W I Z A R D
D . R . T . H . F . . . V
. L O V E L Y . I N D I E
T . F . R . S . A . O . R
W H I L E . S U B J E C T
I . T . D . O . L . R . S
G U S H . A P P E A S E .
```

106

```
P . I . P . K . R . K . S
S U N R I S E . E X I S T
Y . S . R . E . J . W . E
C H I N A . P R O F I L E
H . G . T . . . I . . . R
. . I N T E R M I N A B L E
S . I . . . O . . . I . D
H E A D Q U A R T E R S .
O . U . . . U . T . . . A
W E L C O M E . R E H A B
B . A . T . N . T . D . B
I M B U E . V O L C A N O
Z . S . D . Y . E . Y . T
```

107

```
. A C C O R D S . P E A K
J . L . U . E . H . H . .
E X A M S . C I T I Z E N
L . R . T . E . A . A . .
L O I N . U N S T E A D Y
Y . F . T . T . T . D . .
. S I G H T . W O O D S .
. E . I . F . O . I . S .
U N D E R L I E . A C H E
. E . S . D . A . T . C .
A W A I T E D . Q U I E T
. E . L . L . U . V . S .
T R E K . D E B A T E D .
```

108

```
D I S M A L . W I S H E D
. C . I . U . O . H . Y .
J I N X . N E W C O M E R
. E . T . C . . . V . B .
T R O U G H . P R E F A B
. . R . T . E . . . L . .
M E Z E . I O N . S O L E
. Q . . . M . A . C . . .
N U A N C E . L O O K E D
. A . A . . . T . R . X .
G L A D I O L I . I O T A
. L . I . D . E . N . R .
H Y B R I D . S I G N A L
```

Solutions

109

```
  R A I N B O W   E M I R
A   L   E   X     A     I
C L O S E L Y   J E E R S
A   H   D   G   O   S   K
D W A R F   E Q U A T E
E     U   N   R   R   P
M A I N L Y   S N O O Z E
Y   L   N   M     A     R
  F L E E C E   L O A N S
E   N   S   N   I   R   I
V E E R S   D E S I G N S
E     S     E   T   U   T
N O S E   O D Y S S E Y
```

110

```
    O   Q   C   K   R   M
  T R A U M A   A L I B I
    A   I   R E V   F   N
A B L A Z E     A F F I X
C   S     S   Q   E   M
T E C H N O   U N Z I P
S   O   B O A     N   U
  K N A V E   D I N N E R
  O   C   Y     U   G
F I L E D   J U N G L E
I   Y   O F F   G   L
T H R O W   A S L E E P
S   E   N   X   Y   E
```

111

```
    B   S   B   H   C   F
A L U M N I   Y E L L O W
    O   O   K   P   A   R
S W I G   I N H E R I T S
    O   N   E   I   E
Q U E S T I O N I N G
  T   H     E   K
    D O C U M E N T I N G
E   U   N   L     O
E X P L O D E D   J A C K
  C   D   U   E   O   K
R E V E A L   S E I Z E D
  L   R   Y   T   N   D
```

112

```
  C H E M I S T   J O K E
S   A   A   E   A   P   A
T O N I G H T   F L A W S
A   D   N   T   F   Q   Y
S T Y L I   E Y E F U L
H   F   E   C   E   V
E X O T I C   S T E R E O
D   R   C   S   I   L
  D I V E R T   O C T E T
I   E   N   U   N   W   A
C Y N I C   B L A Z I N G
E   T   E   B   T   C   E
S A S S   T Y P E S E T
```

113

```
N E R D   I   Q   B L A H
O   E   E N S U E   O   I
P A P A   V   O   J O C K
E   S I Z E   T E A K   E
  A   D   S U E   D   B
A C C E P T   S W E A R S
H   I     A   A   A
G E L A T O   D R A I N S
  D   X   T A U   T   D
A   R I C H   T R O Y   S
B I O S   E   I   M A S T
L   O   B R I E F   W   A
Y A K S   S   S   U S E R
```

114

```
A   F   M   H   B   T   F
S Q U E E Z E   U S H E R
I   R   D   R   R   O   E
D E L T A   E X E C U T E
E   O   L   A     I
  S U B S T I T U T I O N
P   G   L     N   G
R E H A B I L I T A T E
O   E   E   E   E   B
B E J E W E L   N U R S E
L   E   A   N   V   R
E R R O R   P R I V A C Y
M   K   E   S   S   L   L
```

115

116

117

118

119

120

Solutions

121

```
MEMO _ M _ F _ USED
A  I _ DEVIL _ H _ U
GANG _ A _ S _ KELP
E _ IRON _ HEAD _ E
_ Q _ O _ IRE _ N _ C
JUNGLE _ SCALES
E _ E _ _ U _ D
TRIVIA _ ABIDES
Y _ I _ FAX _ F _ D
I _ DEAF _ INFO _ S
DRAW _ A _ O _ YUCK
E _ Z _ FILMS _ C _ I
APED _ R _ S _ WHIP
```

122

```
_ H _ M _ C _ S _ J _ S
MASALA _ HEARTH
_ I _ L _ SPY _ I _ U
FREEZE _ L _ LADS
_ D _ _ STY _ _ I
KOALA _ A _ ACTOR
_ S _ HABIT _ A
SEPIA _ L _ EQUAL
_ N _ _ REF _ _ W
SCAB _ E _ EXTRAS
_ O _ E _ PIT _ R _ I
GRAVEL _ EXALTS
_ E _ Y _ Y _ D _ M _ S
```

123

```
_ ADS _ _ BED _ C
_ R _ OKRA _ ICED
TOFU _ _ YEN _ L
_ M _ TOSS _ IDLE
RASH _ Q _ N _ ODE
I _ EMU _ EGO _ G
DOOR _ ION _ BUYS
D _ NUB _ SIS _ U
ADD _ N _ U _ EXAM
SONS _ JEER _ M
_ Z _ ADO _ VIAL
LEAF _ WIPE _ S
N _ EEL _ DOS
```

124

```
_ T _ P _ O _ A _ S _ N
DAHLIA _ QUITE
_ C _ O _ FLU _ L _ X
CROWDS _ ABORT
A _ A _ W _ I _ A
FABRIC _ IRONY
E _ A _ ZAG _ I _ J
_ PASTA _ SVELTE
_ S _ K _ R _ E _ S
RIGID _ DIKTAT
I _ U _ ALP _ C _ R
COYPU _ ATOMIC
H _ S _ B _ D _ N _ P
```

125

```
_ I _ Q _ D _ G _ R _ A
INRUSH _ UNEASY
_ S _ A _ A _ I _ V _ K
STUD _ RENDERED
_ A _ _ M _ E _ A _ W
UNSPEAKABLE
_ T _ R _ _ E _ A
_ FORESHADOWS
P _ M _ X _ I _ E
COMPETED _ JUST
L _ T _ E _ D _ A _ O
FALLEN _ ENZYME
R _ Y _ D _ N _ Z _ E
```

126

```
PALL _ R _ C _ TEST
A _ O _ GENIE _ X _ A
YEAH _ V _ N _ JINX
S _ FOCI _ EMIT _ I
_ B _ U _ ELM _ B _ U
NARROW _ AMENDS
_ T _ R _ _ O _ D
SHARES _ LOUDER
_ S _ E _ KOI _ N _ R
S _ WADI _ QUIZ _ K
PEAR _ L _ U _ TOTE
O _ R _ CLAIM _ N _ G
TIDY _ S _ D _ WEBS
```

127

D	B		C	F		J	F		A
W	E	L	F	A	R	E		U	N	I	O	N
E		A		L		E	N		Z		G
E	X	C	E	L		D	R	I	Z	Z	L	E
B		K	U			U		O			R
	C	O	N	S	I	D	E	R	A	B	L	E
I		U			U			R		D
M	I	T	O	C	H	O	N	D	R	I	A
P				H		R		G		P
R	E	V	E	A	L	S		O	T	H	E	R
E		A		N		L		G		T		A
S	P	R	I	G		E	Q	U	A	L	L	Y
S		Y		E		D		E		Y		S

128

	A		A		G		O		F
S	U	P	E	R		R	U	B	B	E	R
T		P		R	A		V		N		E
R	E	R	E	A	D	S		I	N	D	E	X
A		O		Y		P	O		O		T
W	E	A	N		P		F	U	T	U	R	E
B		C		J	O	K	E	S		N		R
E	C	H	O	E	D		Z		U	D	O	N
R			A		S		M		E		A
R	I	V	A	L		Q	U	A	R	R	E	L
Y		E		O		U		R		L		L
	T	R	A	U	M	A		S	C	A	L	Y
	B		S		D		H		Y

129

S	T	A	R	E	D		B		Y	E	T
	O		U		O		W	O	V	E		E
E	X	P	E	C	T	S		A		S	K	A
	I		U		H	A	S		N
S	C	H	E	R	Z	O		T	R	I	A	L
A		U		S		E		E		V
D	E	G	R	E	E		T	O	F	F	E	E
	Q		U		M		W		L		N
J	U	N	T	A		A	N	N	O	Y	E	D
	I			L	U	G		E			N
S	P	A		O		I	N	D	U	C	E	D
U		S	O	N	G		E		P		M
E	L	K		E		E	S	S	A	Y	S

130

Q	U	O	T	E	D		P	O	E	T	I	C
	T		O		I		R		X		N
W	I	S	P		F	L	O	A	T	I	N	G
	L		I		F		F		R		E
D	I	S	C	R	E	T	E		E	U	R	O
	T			R		S		M
Z	Y	G	O	T	E		S	H	E	L	V	E
		P		N		I		E
A	C	H	E		T	R	O	M	B	O	N	E
R		R		I		N		U		T
M	A	H	A	R	A	J	A		R	O	U	T
W		T		T		L		K		R
F	L	E	E	C	E		S	C	A	L	E	D

131

S		E		C		A	E		F		E
Q	U	I	L	L		C	O	M	P	L	E	X
U		G		A		I		P		A		I
A	S	H	A	M	E	D		L	I	K	E	S
S		T		I		O				T
H	I	E	R	A	R	C	H	Y		S	I	S
	E		B			E		W
G	E	N		S	U	F	F	E	R	I	N	G
O			O			R			T		O
V	I	P	E	R		O	B	J	E	C	T	S
E		U		B		Z		E		H		P
R	E	L	I	E	V	E		T	H	E	R	E
N		L		D		N		S		D		L

132

S		C		F		E		J	A		E
C	O	O	K	I	N	G		A	N	N	E	X
A		I		A		G		G		T		P
L	I	F	T	S		S	Q	U	E	E	Z	E
E		F		C			A			N
	D	E	M	O	N	S	T	R	A	T	E	S
A		U			A			W		E
B	U	R	E	A	U	C	R	A	T	I	C
S			L			R		L		B
O	V	E	R	M	A	N		T	R	I	B	E
R		G		O		O		F		G		R
B	O	O	T	S		D	O	U	G	H	T	Y
S		S		T		S		L		T		L

133

```
. E D I T I O N . S L O W
B . I . R . P . . E . Z .
A I S L E . E Q U A T O R
N . A . K . R . N . N . .
J A B S . C A P T U R E D
O . L . W . S . U . E . .
. P I X I E . A C U T E .
. N . N . A . K . R . H .
O R G A N I Z E . L I R A
E . E . A . O . E . R . .
L I B E R A L . M O V E D
. G . M . . E . I . A . Y
I N F O . E A R T H L Y .
```

134

```
. G . A . F . N . M . H .
L O U N G E . I V O R Y .
. L . T . Z I G . O . M .
A F F A I R . . H E R O N
L . W . . W . L . I . . .
A B J E C T . O F F A L .
S . A . . I R K . D . S .
. B R I D E . E X P O R T
. O . N . S . . L . . E .
H A C K S . . A N Y H O W
Y . O . T A N . A . A . .
P A S H A . U N I Q U E .
E . H . B . N . L . L . .
```

135

```
F I E S T A . S P E A K S
. G . I . M . I . V . N .
F L E X . B A C H E L O R
. O . T . I . R . W . . .
O O Z I N G . S T Y M I E
. . E . U . O . . N . . .
J O Y S . I L L . W A G S
. P . . T . I . A . . . .
S T U M P Y . C U R S O R
. I . O . . I . P . U . .
A C Q U A I N T . I O T A
. A . S . N . O . N . D .
S L E E P S . R E G I O N
```

136

```
. R . A . R . S . I . P .
L E N G T H . W A R I L Y
. C . E . I C E . K . A .
C O U S I N . E . S A Y S
U . . O F T . . E . . . .
S P O O F . U . E V A D E
. R . A N N O Y . R . . .
Q U E S T . G . E X C E L
N . . Z I P . . J . . . .
S C U D . E . A N T H E M
L . U . B U G . U . C . .
M A T T E R . E I G H T H
D . Y . A . D . S . S . .
```

137

```
. J . R E Q U E S T . R .
A U R A . U . A . O K A Y
. N . C H A R T E R . Z .
B I L E . L . E . C H E W
. O . . I N N S . E . O .
C R A B . F . . A F A R .
O . C O P Y R I G H T . D
M I T T . . M . A Y E S .
E . O . S W A P . . X . .
T A R N . R . R . C L E F
. C . A X O L O T L . M .
S N A P . N . V . O O P S
. E . S U G G E S T . T .
```

138

```
. B A F F L E D . J A C K
E . N . O . N . . E . R .
Q U A I L . C H A T E A U
U . L . K . O . F . Z . .
I C O N . P R E F I X E D
P . G . P . E . O . Y . .
. F O O L S . T R U L Y .
. U . A . V . D . O . D .
O B S E S S E D . S P E W
A . M . N . I . H . E . .
S K Y W A R D . S C O W L
E . A . E . L . N . L . .
O D D S . A D H E R E S .
```

Solutions

139

```
 C D S   I T   J
A L K A L I   N E R V E
 A T   P I C   A   E
C Y M B A L   H Y P E R
A   E   Z E O
L E V E L S   O F T E N
L   I   W O O   R   K
 B A Y O U   S Q U A R E
 I   E   M   S   E
H O R S E   E L E V E N
O   O   U P S   I   I
A F T E R   A D V I C E
X   I   O   G   E   E
```

140

```
 R J G   S V   O
P E L O T A   A X I O M S
 A W   T   F   O   E
I D O L   E N A B L I N G
 E   A   R   E   S
P R E C A U T I O N S
 S   H   C   D
 P A R E N T H E S E S
V   S   F   A   N
W A S T E F U L   A K I N
 G   I   O   E   Q   Z
G U I T A R   N A U S E A
 E   Y   T   T   A   N
```

141

```
 R I B C A G E   U D O N
A T   O   E   E   O
V A C A N C Y   R A D I O
O   H   S   S   A   U   K
C O Y P U   E F F E C T
A   L   R   F   E   V
D I L A T E   M I D D L E
O   O   A   A   S   S
 W A R N E D   H E E L S
Z   D   C   J   N   X   E
E D I F Y   U N E Q U A L
S   N   S   S   D   S
T O G S   S T A S H E D
```

142

```
P U F F   E   C   A S K S
A E   S Q U I D   P   H
T U T U   U   T   C I A O
H   A R E A   I R O N   W
 D   G   T O E   M   D
F R E E Z E   S T A Y E D
O   I   I   B
T O M A T O   E N T I T Y
 L   J   F A X   W   S
I   H A L F   P A I D   E
D O O R   E   O   N A V Y
L   G   C R U S H   U   E
E A S Y   S   E   E B B S
```

143

```
 P D R   H   P S
H A I R D O   O G L I N G
 T   A   S I N   O   O
D I K T A T   E   T H O U
 N   I V Y   Z
M A N I A   O   E A S E L
 I   T W I R L   K
S O L V E   L   F L I E S
 X   J A B   X
E Y E D   O   L O C A T E
 G   O   L E I   O   E
S E Q U E L   M O M E N T
 N   R   Y   P   B   T
```

144

```
L E A V E   G U E S S E S
 A   I   L   N   A   J
B R O C C O L I   L E E S
 T   E   C   V   S   C
D H A R M A   E X A C T
 O   L   R   E
V A R Y   I N S   W I D E
 C   Z   I   H
 Q U O T A   T R I C K Y
 U   T   T   I   S   O
P I N T   I D E N T I F Y
 R   E   O   S   L   T
W E A R I N G   M E T A L
```

145

```
  S B N   Q W   O
P E S E T A   U N I T Y
  E A   P H I   S   E
C A M P U S     T O P A Z
L   S     V   A   I
A L B I N O   I N F E R
D   O   N I B     M   U
  T A T T Y   E N J O Y S
  A   O   X     O     E
D R A W N     B U T T E R
O   B   E N D   R   R
T H E T A   R A N G E D
E   T   T   Y   S   K
```

146

```
  R E Q U I R E   O V A L
B   X   L   E     W   D
L A T I N   A C C L A I M
A   E   A   S   A     E
D U N G   D O U B T F U L
E   S   H   N   L   A
  L I V E S   K E T C H
    V   R   O   S   T   I
C L E A N E R S   J O Y S
  O   I   A   S   R   L
O V E R A L L   P R I Z E
  E   A   L   E   E   S
T R O D   E Y E W A S H
```

147

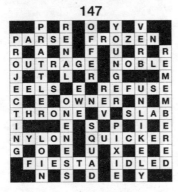

```
  P R   O   Y   V
P A R S E   F R O Z E N
R   A   N   F   U   R   R
O U T R A G E   N O B L E
J   T   L   R   G     M
E E L S   E   R E F U S E
C   E   O W N E R   N   M
T H R O N E   V   S L A B
I   E   S   P   I   E
N Y L O N   Q U I C K E R
G   O   E   U   X   E   E
  F I E S T A   I D L E D
  N   S   D   E   Y
```

148

```
B A H T   E   P   S T O W
A   O   S Q U I B   R   A
B L O C   U   Z   O I L Y
E   F O C I   Z E R O   S
  X   N   P E A   C   J
V E R S U S   S T A T E D
N   N   R   A   A   W
D O M I N O   C U R V E S
  N   R   B A A   U   L
T   D I E T   U G L Y   E
A G E S   A   G   E A T S
L   W   F I G H T   W   P
K E Y S   N   T   I N K Y
```

149

```
A B S O R B S   L E A S E
  A   V   I   J   L   Y
E N T E R T A I N M E N T
  N   R   E   G     T
K E Y W O R D S   C H A T
  D   H     A   O   X
  R E V I E W I N G
C   L   T     F   S
F I R M   A D E Q U A T E
T     L   R   S   A
O R G A N I Z A T I O N S
  I   H   C   S   O   C
S C R A P   P E N N I E S
```

150

```
  S O W   B E E   Q
  T   I D E A   N O U N
W R I T   R U T   A
  I   H Y M N   E V I L
A P E D   A   R   L A Y
U   R A J   A S K   S
K A V A   O H M   N O T E
X   W A R   A G O   V
F L U   C   Z   C O M E
E P I C   L E E K   E
  E   U S E   I O N S
O N U S   A M E N   D
  D   E E K   G A S
```

Solutions

151

```
. P R O D U C T . . N E E D
A . E . A . R . . I . . X .
R U S T Y . A Z A L E A S .
I . P . S . T . S . . L . .
S K E W . R E F L E C T S .
E . C . B . R . E . O . . .
. S T E A M . W E E N Y . .
. E . R . C . P . T . K . .
U N D E R L I E . J I B E .
. E . E . R . G . N . E . .
T I T A N I C . E Q U I P .
. G . M . . L . N . A . S .
C H O P . R E V E A L S . .
```

152

```
A B B E Y S . S . R I G
. E . L . A . S H A H . E
J A C K E T S . R . O F T
. U . Q . E M U . . L .
E X E C U T E . B O N U S
A . T . A . D . V . T .
R E A L L Y . A M A Z E S
. D . I . C . I . O . K
V I P E R . H I S T O R Y
. C . E . E G O . T . A
A T E . T . W A S T I N G
S . M I R E . L . W . G
P R O . O . . P H O N E D
```

153

```
S N E A K Y . I S O M E R
E . V . E . H . U . O . E
Q U E S T I O N S . A R M
U . N . C . U . H . N . E
E A T . H O R R I F I E D
L . . U . S . . N . Y
. H E L P S . W E I G H .
S . M . . S . Y . . . J
E S P I O N A G E . E R A
L . O . Z . F . B . X . U
D E W . O P E R A T I O N
O . E . N . S . L . L . T
M A R K E T . A L I E N S
```

154

```
B E L I E F . C L I M B S
. X . M . I . A . D . A
Q U I P . R E P L Y I N G
. D . U . E . . . L . N
F E L L O W . F I L M I C
. S . O . I . . . N .
K N E E . R A N . J O G S
. O . . K . I . O . .
E V I C T S . S E I Z E D
. E . I . . H . N . R
G L A D I O L I . T R O T
. T . E . D . N . L . D
H Y B R I D . G E Y S E R
```

155

```
. W . O . C . V . M . R
J O Y F U L . A Z A L E A
. R . F . A . L . C . P
S K I S . U N U S A B L E
E . . S . E . R . Y .
P R O G R E S S I O N .
. S . E . . . N . O
. U N C O N S C I O U S .
. A . E . R . I . . T
Q U I T T I N G . T O S H
. R . I . E . H . E . I
F A L C O N . T U X E D O
. L . S . T . S . T . E
```

156

```
. S W E A T E D . I S L E
O . O . C . V . . . A . Y
B A R O Q U E . I N D I E
J . S . U . N . G . N . D
E X T R A . T I N T E D .
C . . I . S . O . S . F
T E C H N O . E R A S E R
S . O . T . A . A . . E
. O P T I N G . M A G I C
I . Y . N . E . U . L . K
F L I N G . I N S T A L L
F . N . . S . E . Z . E
Y O G I . S T A S H E D
```

157

U	S	A	B	L	E		I		F	O	P
	A		A		Y		J	O	K	E	
Q	U	E	R	I	E	S		N		Z	A	G
	N		T		C	H	I			X	
T	A	B	L	E	A	U		C	H	A	I	N
A		Y		M	D			I		O	
G	R	E	A	S	Y		I	N	C	O	M	E
	E		H		B		A		A		W
O	S	C	A	R		O	B	S	E	R	V	E
	E		I	L	L		A			I	
S	T	Y	S		S		D	E	L	A	Y	E	D
U		E	V	E	R		G		I		W
N	E	T		S		O	L	D	E	S	T

158

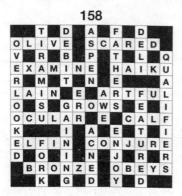

159

S	O	F	T		D		J		A	Q	U	A
I		L		L	E	G	A	L		U		I
Z	E	A	L		C		C		D	I	E	D
E		W	I	K	I		K	N	I	T		S
	I		R		D	U	E		L		S	
U	N	S	A	F	E		T	A	L	K	I	E
	A		U			S		X		X	
E	N	T	I	R	E		S	H	E	E	T	S
	E		D		M	O	O		B		H	
A		G	L	O	B		R	I	B	S		U
S	W	A	Y		E		T		S	I	T	S
P		V		A	D	D	E	R		F		E
S	U	E	S		S		D		S	T	U	D

160

161